Lea

IQ

EMMETT C. MURPHY

John Wiley & Sons, Inc.

New York ➤ Chichester ➤ Weinheim ➤ Brisbane ➤ Singapore ➤ Toronto

To Carol

Copyright © 1996 by Emmett C. Murphy
Published by John Wiley & Sons, Inc.

First Wiley mass market edition published 1997

Library of Congress Cataloging-in-Publication Data

Murphy, Emmett C.
    Leadership IQ : a personal development process based on a scientific study of a new generation of leaders / Emmett C. Murphy.
         p.   cm.
    Includes bibliographical references and index.
    ISBN 0-471-14712-5 (cloth)
    ISBN 0-471-19327-5 (mass market)
    1. Leadership.   2. Management.   I. Title.
HD57.7.M87   1996
658.4'092—dc20   96-14172
                                           CIP

Printed in the United States of America
10 9 8 7 6 5 4 3 2 1

Contents

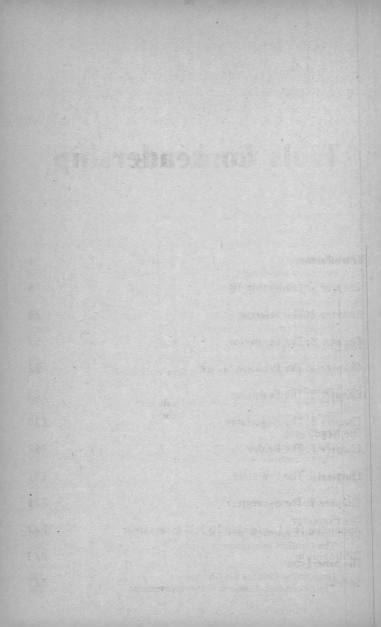

Tools for Leadership

Acknowledgments

This book grew out of our firm's consulting work and research with several hundred business, healthcare, government, and public service organizations. While they and the many outstanding leaders who lead them must go largely unnamed, my colleagues at E. C. Murphy, Ltd., and I want to express our deep appreciation for their inspiration and partnership throughout the project.

A central objective of the Leadership IQ project was the development of a new generation of leadership, assessment, and development tools that will meet the exciting but often difficult challenges of the new economy. I want to thank Mark Murphy, my son and intellectual partner, for heading up this effort and making key contributions to the manuscript.

I owe special thanks to my agent and creative partner Michael Snell, who helped me to distill a reasonably economical and coherent manuscript from a mountain of research data. Michael and I have shared journeys like this before with two other books, *The Genius of Sitting Bull: 13 Heroic Strategies for Today's Business Leaders* and *Forging the Heroic Organization*. My admiration and respect for Michael's manuscript development skills grow with each effort. My gratitude also goes to Patricia Snell for her gracious hospitality and support during formative design sessions.

I also want to extend a heartfelt thank you to Janet Coleman, Senior Editor at John Wiley and Sons, for her friendly encouragement, penetrating insight into the substance of the book, and creative shaping of its structure.

The concept of Leadership IQ was also greatly influenced by the diagnostic insights of the professionals at E. C. Murphy, Ltd. While I cannot thank them all here, I want to express special appreciation to Jim Pepicello, Jayne Carson, Patrick Garland, Connie Paxson, Shirley Ruch, John Sheehan, Jim Turner, Linda Buchanan, and Sharon DeJoy. Throughout the project I was also ably assisted by two research associates, Amy Penasack and Andrea Burgio. Amy oversaw the assembly and copyediting of the manuscript with creative professionalism and Andrea provided insightful scholarship in the areas of research design and assessment. My thanks also go to Kelly Schuler and Mary Kanick for picking up the pieces often left behind.

The book has its conceptual roots in the works of several scholarly friends, most notably Ed Schein, Bill Glasser, and Joseph Alutto. To each, thank you.

Most of all, I want to express my thanks to my wife Carol, to whom I dedicate this book, for her unfailing love and support, and also to our daughter Marissa, the first violinist in our family quartet.

Introduction

■ INTELLIGENT LEADERSHIP

Today's world may have [leaders], but they are now overshadowed by celebrities: The [leader] is known for achievements . . ., the celebrity for well-knownness. The [leader] reveals the possibilities of human nature, the celebrity reveals the possibilities of the press and the media. Celebrities are people who make the news, but [leaders] are people who make history.

—DANIEL BOORSTIN
Parade magazine, 8/6/95

Our research and consulting firm, E. C. Murphy, Ltd., has been dedicated for over twenty years to one central purpose: scientifically investigating the nature of leadership and work in an ever-changing economy. Five years ago, as an outgrowth of this effort, we launched a comprehensive empirical study to identify the characteristics and talents of leaders who, as Daniel Boorstin observes, make history. These are the people to whom others turn when missions need to be upheld, breakthroughs made, and performance goals reached on time and within budget. These are the leaders who transcend the problems of the moment to reveal the possibilities of human nature through intelligence and perseverance.

Identifying and developing such leaders has never been more challenging than it is today. For the United States, steeped in the tradition of Jefferson, Lincoln, and Roosevelt, the age of great leaders seems to have passed. As we look to Washington, Wall Street, and corporate boardrooms for leadership, we find ourselves intensely questioning the capacity of contemporary society to produce leaders with sufficient intelligence and resolve to meet the challenges of the twenty-first century. In spite of the brilliance of such individual leaders as Bill Gates and Jack Welch, we question whether we will find a body of leaders sufficient to move our large and complex society to a new level of progress and maturity.

■ THE GOOD NEWS

This book brings the good news that the answer to this question is *yes*. A new generation of exceptionally able leaders is emerging from every level and sector of society. These leaders are already renewing the energy and resolve of a society that has been laboring under the burdens of self doubt, debt, and self-interest. At a time when the view from Washington can be discouraging, this book provides a view from the front lines of a society moving forward with optimism and purpose. And, at a time when the media record the failure of leadership through ineptness and selfishness, our new research uncovers seven important discoveries that confirm the intelligence and commitment of a new generation of leadership genius.

■ THE FINDINGS

The *first* and most basic discovery is that leadership can be defined and measured as a form of intelligence. For too long, the concept of leadership has been addressed through anecdotes, hearsay, and self-aggrandizing discussion. While virtually every other system of our society and economy has gone through rigorous empirical analysis, leadership has remained at a relatively primitive level of study—until now. This book is driven by the findings of a comprehensive and in-depth study that sets a new benchmark for analysis and self-improvement.

Second, while conventional wisdom tends to separate the people working in an organization—be it Chase Manhattan Bank, Massachusetts General Hospital, Wal-Mart, or the U.S. Defense Intelligence Agency—into two distinct and separate categories, those who work and those who lead, we learned that in a successful organization *every leader works and every worker leads.* History supports this conclusion. Thomas Jefferson worked as an architect and inventor, designing the University of Virginia and fabricating the most effective plan of his time, and led his country as its third president. Mohandas Gandhi led an entire nation to independence and worked as a lawyer defending civil rights in South Africa.

As we analyzed our research into the beliefs and practices of more than 18,000 contemporary leaders in 562 business, healthcare, and public service organizations in the United States, Canada, Mexico, and Asia, 1,029 individuals emerged who Boorstin might consider authentic leaders— people admired by their superiors, peers, and subordinates as highly effective. Working in every kind of organization, from multinational corporations and regional healthcare providers to small businesses and local, state and federal government, these 1,029 people represent every level of leadership, from warehouse clerk to CEO. We came to call them *workleaders,* a term that binds work and leadership in a way that reflects the true nature of effective leadership. In this book you will meet dozens of them, who prove by their words and actions that every leader works and every worker leads.

We gained a *third* important insight when we saw another consistent pattern in the behavior of workleaders: they know how to say the right thing to the right people at the right time to get the right work done well, on time, and within budget. While they reveal themselves by their deeds and thus provide role models for everyone with whom they interact, as Sam Walton did for every Wal-Mart associate, they also reveal themselves through their words. They have mastered the *art of conversation*. As we eavesdropped on their conversations with the stakeholders in their organizations—a high-tech marketing manager talking with a recently hired sales associate, a cardiac care nurse conversing with her supervisor, a team of municipal council members discussing economic development with local businesspeople—we saw that they follow well-crafted *scripts* in all of their communications. In the chapters that follow you will see real people using real scripts in real situations, and you will learn how to adapt them to your own work environment.

Workleading is both an art and a science, but contrary to the traditional notion that leaders are born and not made, anyone can *learn* to be a workleader. This *fourth* insight arose as our research uncovered the fact that workleaders rely on specific *tools* to fulfill eight specific *roles*. In every case, workleaders know how to

➤ *Select the right people*

➤ *Connect them to the right cause*

➤ *Solve problems that arise*

➤ *Evaluate progress towards objectives*

➤ *Negotiate resolutions to conflicts*

➤ *Heal the wounds inflicted by change*

➤ *Protect their cultures from the perils of crisis*

➤ *Synergize all stakeholders in a way that enables them to achieve improvement together*

Each of this book's chapters on these eight workleader roles presents two practical tools from our research findings that you can put to immediate use in your own work life.

Our conclusion about roles and tools led to our *fifth*, and perhaps most valuable, insight: When workleaders master the eight roles, they achieve what we call a *synergistic kick*. While the role of the synergizer reflects a specific skill in and of itself, it also serves as a supervening discipline. When workleaders master it and infuse it into the other seven roles, it ignites a chain reaction where one-plus-seven roles no longer equal eight, but create a state of achievement far beyond what individuals, teams, and organizations ever dreamed possible. In the first chapter we explore this synergistic kick in some detail because we feel strongly that you should understand, before you begin studying the individual roles, that it represents the ultimate goal toward which all workleaders strive.

Our *sixth* insight came about as we administered and refined a research instrument we call *Work Imaging*™. Dedicated from the outset to going beyond the sort of limited, anecdotal research into work and leadership that informs so much of what is written on the subject, we developed a comprehensive and detailed survey technique that allows us and our clients to obtain a clear picture of precisely what workleaders and their associates do every day. The results of an individual's Work Imaging serve two purposes. First, they enable a workleader to perform an accurate self-assessment; second, they provide a precise understanding of how to help associates refocus their responsibilities and efforts. Workleaders and their teams are twice as focused on their key role responsibilities as average leaders and their organizations. For example, a sales associate in a retail bicycle shop might say her job description requires her to spend 75 percent of her time in direct contact with customers, and she may think she actually spends 67 percent of her time achieving that goal, but her Work Imaging shows that she actually spends only 38 percent in direct contact with customers. With that information in hand, her workleader can help her redesign her work role to close the gap between the 75 percent goal and the 38 percent reality. This process takes the guesswork out of performance, separates myth from reality, and provides a pathway to higher achievement. We have distilled the sophisticated Work Imaging diagnostic process into a basic set of problem-solving tools included in this book.

■ GETTING STARTED

To start on this self-improvement process, we urge you to take the Leadership IQ Self-Assessment (LIQ) in the appendix. The LIQ measures your present understanding of the key competencies required for high Leadership IQ. This is followed by a Development Guide that targets specific chapters and sections of the book for self-improvement. To gain insight into the landmark research and guiding principles that frame the whole issue of Leadership IQ, read Chapter 1. And for further information on the ongoing research and self-improving tools being developed to improve Leadership IQ, call E. C. Murphy, Ltd. regarding the Leadership IQ Research Project at 1-800-922-5005 or contact us on the Internet at emurph02@interserv.com.

Our *seventh* insight occurred last, as we mulled over all that had occurred while we worked shoulder-to-shoulder with the 1,029 workleaders on whom we focused most of our attention: They obey Seven Guiding Principles in everything they do and say.

1. Be an achiever
2. Be pragmatic
3. Practice strategic humility
4. Be customer-focused
5. Be committed
6. Be a learned optimist
7. Be responsible

These principles form the bedrock upon which workleaders build an architecture of achievement. We discuss them in Chapter 1.

Saint James said, "Faith, if it has no works, is dead." More than anything, our investigation affirms that faith still flourishes among workleaders, a generation of high achievers who have thrown off cynicism and selfishness to make masterpieces of their personal and work lives. Their unending quest for meaning and achievement can inspire us all to improve our Leadership IQ.

1

Leadership IQ

Five years ago, as my colleagues and I launched the formal research that would result in this book, I recalled a story that I had once heard Eleanor Roosevelt tell. I grew up in Hyde Park, New York, the Roosevelts' home town, and was honored to have the opportunity of studying the qualities of American leadership with Mrs. Roosevelt as part of a special program for high school students. During one session, she told the following story.

> *The mythological hero Aeneas was once asked to judge a contest between four archers. Each one was told to aim at a dove tethered to the top of a pole. The first archer stepped forward and didn't even try for the dove, but took dead aim on the pole and hit it. The second tried for the dove but his arrow went astray and severed the tether instead. As the dove rose in flight, the third hit it squarely with his arrow. Then, without hesitation, the fourth archer stepped forward and shot his arrow into the sky, where it burst into flames and disappeared into the heavens.*
>
> *So to which archer would you give the prize? Aeneas answered the question by awarding fourth prize to the archer who tried for the dove but hit the tether. That archer was like the leader who reaches beyond his abilities, tries to show off and instead creates a mess. Third prize went to the archer who hit the pole. He knew his limits and worked within them. Second prize went to the archer who hit the dove. He accom-*

plished his goal. But Aeneas admired most the archer who reached for the sky, because he knew how to do more than just hit the target—he knew how to show the way.

Mrs. Roosevelt went on to say that she and President Roosevelt had often spoken about the remarkable ability of our society to produce archers whose work soars beyond the imagination of others, archers like Thomas Jefferson, Abraham Lincoln, and—while she was too modest to point this out—perhaps herself and her husband.

■ LEADERSHIP INTELLIGENCE

Mindful of that story, my colleagues and I began our search for contemporary Americans who deserve first prize in the contest for leadership excellence, those workleaders who, in the eyes of their peers, subordinates, and superiors, work and lead beyond the imaginations of others. In the end, the study identified 1,029 people who demonstrate an exceptional level of leadership intelligence, what Webster defines as the ability to "show the way":

> *The degree to which a leader is able to use the faculty of reason—the ability to learn from experience, to otherwise acquire and retain knowledge and to respond successfully to new situations—to guide or show others to an effective course of action or thought.*
>
> —From *Webster's New World Dictionary of the American Language*, 1990, On leadership and intelligence

The research fleshed out this definition to identify the content of Leadership Intelligence: the knowledge and skills that enable a leader to use the faculty of reason to guide others to a successful course of action. These results are distilled in this book.

▓ THE SEARCH FOR LEADERSHIP IQ

The search for leaders with high Leadership IQ was driven by a simple pattern of recognition. Wherever we went, whether to large or small businesses, hospitals, or governmental and public service agencies, we invariably found that people at all levels and in all types of roles consistently referred us to the same few individuals when we asked such questions as: Who are the most effective leaders in this organization? To whom do people turn for guidance in difficult situations? And to whom would you turn if you needed results?

Everyone we asked in a given situation, whether a board member, vice president, customer, front-line worker, or CEO, would invariably single out the same two or three leaders. It became clear that, regardless of organizational politics and economic pressures, everyone recognized outstanding work-leaders when they saw them. This fact came across vividly when the president of a hospital observed, "Though I don't like her very much, and though she can give me a hard time over priorities, the most effective leader in this place is Jo Ostrowski, manager of the oncology product line. I would, and have, trusted her with the lives of my family. No person, procedure, or operational problem is going to stop her from getting results for her patients."

After a few months of gathering names like Jo Ostrowski, my associates and I established a more formal and far-reaching research protocol to seek out workleaders recognized as exceptionally competent by subordinates, peers, and superiors (though not necessarily immediate superiors, who—unfortunately—quite frequently feel intimidated by high-performing subordinates). Representatives of all ranks of an organization must, we decided, independently and consistently recommend a person for us to include him or her in our population of exceptional workleaders.

Once we had pinpointed 1,029 exceptional workleaders, we set upon the task of determining what, if anything, sets them apart from others. We used a variety of assessment tools, ranging from psychological inventories and customer satisfaction assessments, to work productivity and performance measures. The results verified that leaders selected by their colleagues as superior performers also produce superior levels of customer satisfaction, productivity, and financial performance. The testing also established that superior performers approach people and their work much differently than others. With these conclusions in mind, we developed the *Leadership IQ Self-Assessment* to delve more deeply into the knowledge, skills, and behaviors that contribute to the development of outstanding Leadership Intelligence.

From the results of our Leadership IQ Self-Assessment we were gradually able to build a *Leadership IQ Development Guide*, a comprehensive leadership selection, assessment, and development tool that anyone can use to boost Leadership IQ and join the ranks of the workleaders. (A basic version designed to correspond with this book is included in the appendix.) This enabled us to go beyond subjective impressions to a much more objective and comprehensive understanding of what makes workleaders tick. As one CEO put it, "If I'm going to stake my career and my company's survival on the performance of others, I want to select and develop people based on legitimate, scientifically verifiable standards, not the advice of some self-proclaimed expert."

■ THE RESULTS

As the research results rolled in, an intriguing profile emerged. Out of the general leadership sample, less than six percent were nominated by peers, subordinates, and superiors as exceptional workleaders. These individuals did not statistically differ from others in certain basic personal and professional variables. Rank in the organization, for example, did not predict whether others would cite an individual as possessing high Leadership IQ. Neither a CEO nor a team leader in the front lines held an advantage. Nor did sex, race, or educational background influence the selection.

What did influence the selection was recognition that highly effective leaders follow certain distinct principles and carry out certain precise roles. To understand these principles and roles, we studied our workleader population more closely until we were able to produce a concrete profile of the Seven Guiding Principles that inform high Leadership IQ and the Eight Roles and related skills required to translate those principles into action.

■ THE GUIDING PRINCIPLES

Leaders with high Leadership IQ have mastered the equivalent of a liberal arts education in the practical realities of human behavior. Through trial and error and disciplined study in the front lines of economic and political life they have learned how to make business and society work. Their knowledge is grounded in the Seven Guiding Principles of leadership, which provide the basis for fulfilling the Eight Roles of the workleader. The principles flow logically from each other:

The Seven Guiding Principles

1. Be an achiever
2. Be pragmatic
3. Practice strategic humility
4. Be customer-focused
5. Be committed
6. Learn to be an optimist
7. Accept responsibility

➤ #1. Be an Achiever

> *We can't make a deal, Mr. Goldwyn, because you are mainly interested in art, and I'm only concerned with money.*
>
> —GEORGE BERNARD SHAW,
> when Samuel Goldwyn insisted that he wanted to turn Shaw's
> play *Pygmalion* into an artistic film

Highly effective leaders have learned that self-reliance and personal competence provide the prerequisites to self-respect and success. Believing that success depends on personal achievement in the front lines of service, workleaders understand that *what you know* propels individual progress in a society founded on the ideals of pluralistic democracy. In the new world economy where every leader must work and every worker must lead, the motto becomes, "If I fail, we fail; if we fail, I fail." Workleaders stand in direct opposition to both *celebrity leaders,* who believe that who you know is more important than what you know, and to *money leaders,* who believe Shaw's satirical observation that the key to success is a function of who you can buy or manipulate.

As part of our study, we asked the 1,029 outstanding workleaders to rate the importance of ten key factors that influence individual success at work and in personal life. A random sample of 1,000 leaders from the population at large, which served as a control group, also ranked these ten key factors. The contrast in their priorities (shown in the following box) reveals some striking differences.

By placing individual competence at the top of their list, those with high Leadership IQ indicated their belief that they control their own destinies. The workleaders we studied attributed fully 80 percent of their success to the top five ranked items, all of which relate to their ability to take control of events either through individual expertise or through the ability to inspire confidence and support in others, including customers.

SUCCESS FACTORS	
Workleader Ranking	*Average Leader Ranking*
1. Individual competence	1. Support from the organization
2. Experience in the front lines of service	2. Support from the boss
3. Respect of customers	3. Formal education
4. Respect of colleagues	4. Luck
5. Support of loved ones	5. Other
6. Formal education	6. Respect of customers
7. Support from the organization	7. Individual competence
8. Support from the boss	8. Experience in the front lines of service
9. Other	9. Support of loved ones
10. Luck	10. Respect of colleagues

By contrast, average leaders feel that their fate on the job lies more in the hands of others, as they indicated by ascribing 70 percent of their potential to succeed or fail to four factors—three of which, including *luck,* are beyond their control. Average leaders ranked formal education, and where you got it, third, viewing it as more important than individual work performance, which they ranked seventh. Average leaders believe that success depends more on who you know (support from the organization ranked first, followed by support from the boss) than what you know, while high achievers believe just the opposite. For them, what you know and your ability to use it to the maximum benefit of customers provide the key to success in both life and work.

David McClelland, the American social scientist, noted that civilizations rise and fall based on the belief structures of their people. For people driven by the need for affiliation, advancement devolves into a game of who you know. Societies in which this becomes the dominant motivator inevitably decline as the value of achievement gives way to privilege, and rewards for service to the many give way to rewards for service to the few.

Similarly, for people driven by the need for power, advancement becomes a game of who you can buy or manipulate. Societies in which this becomes the dominant motivator also inevitably decline as the value of achievement gives way to a predatory struggle to eat or be eaten, where the goal is to win at all costs regardless of the consequences for anyone else.

By contrast, people driven by the need for achievement define advancement as a consequence of *what you know and can accomplish*. Societies in which this motivator dominates grow and prosper as achievement leads to progress, and rewards for service to society encourage people to innovate and join with others to improve the common good. The good news for society today is that a new generation of workleaders is emerging to counterbalance the "who you know" and "who you can buy" attitudes that grew so prevalent in the 1980s.

➤ #2. Be Pragmatic

When it came to selecting engineers, Thomas Edison was a pragmatist. He'd give the applicant a light bulb and ask, "How much water will it hold?" Most candidates would calculate the bulb's volume mathematically, an approach that takes twenty minutes or more. The smart ones, however, would fill the bulb with water and then pour its contents into a measuring cup, a procedure that took less than one minute. Which engineer do you think Edison hired?

Like Edison, contemporary workleaders realize that achievement requires pragmatism, a willingness to ask questions and to search openly and without bias for practical answers to the most vexing problems. Workleaders use pragmatic questioning as a core strategy for leadership for two reasons. Grant Walsh, one of our workleader CEOs, explains:

*Questions allow you to research and communicate at the same
time. They not only generate the data you need to make an
informed decision but communicate what you stand for, your
personal commitment to gaining understanding and insight.*

Workleaders are scientists at heart. They've learned, like
the great architect and pragmatist Frank Lloyd Wright, that
form must follow function. They have also learned to experi-
ment and withhold judgment until they have objectively
assessed a situation and identified a well-reasoned course of
action. Such action must then also withstand the scrutiny of
assessment, a process which teaches even the most confident
workleader to practice strategic humility.

➤ **#3. Practice Strategic Humility**

*Too many of the leaders at the top of our government and cor-
porations were born on third base but give themselves credit
for hitting a triple.*

—JOHN KUBASIAK,
workleader, entrepreneur, and immigrant

In his book, *Overdrive: Managing in Crisis-Filled Times,*
Michael Silva tells a story about the risks of pride.

*In the days before radar a Navy battleship was proceeding
cautiously through dense fog when a lookout spotted the lights
of another ship directly in the cruiser's path. The fleet commander ordered the signal man to flash a warning for the
other ship to make way for the cruiser. The offending ship
flashed in response, "Please change your course 20 degrees
port." Incensed, the commander told the signal man to
respond, "I'm a fleet commander, you change your course 20
degrees!" The response: "I am a seaman second class, and I
suggest you change your course 20 degrees port!" By this time,
the fleet commander was livid. Embarrassed by the flash com-*

*munication that everyone on the bridge could see, the com-
mander ordered the following signal: "I command a battleship, it is in your interest to change course." The response
came immediately: "I am the maintenance seaman of a light-
house, and I strongly suggest you change course."*

One of the most interesting qualities displayed by
workleaders is their practice of what we call *strategic humility*. It reinforces the fact that mature, savvy, and intelligent
leaders know what they *don't* know, an understanding that in
turn fuels an almost insatiable appetite to learn. We use the
term *strategic* humility because it results from a strategic
decision to use learning as a tool for progress, and it charac-
terizes confident and assertive leaders. What distinguishes
such well-known figures as Sam Walton and Andy Grove
from others is their recognition of the truth in Igor Stravin-
sky's words: "The awareness of one's ignorance grows expo-
nentially with one's knowledge."

Unlike the fleet commander, workleaders don't let pride
get in the way of thinking, and even if they have been born
on third base, they don't give themselves credit for hitting a
triple but use it as a starting point for their own hitting
streak. Workleaders seek a purpose for leadership beyond
self-interest, which explains why they place the customer at
the center of their concern.

➤ #4. Be Customer-Focused

Service to others is the rent you pay for your room here on earth.

—MUHAMMAD ALI

Throughout our study, workleaders consistently demonstrated a more intense commitment to shared contribution
and service than average- and low-performing leaders. This

led us to conduct a special study in which we asked 412 control group leaders and 387 workleaders to draw a picture of their concept of leadership by inserting themselves into a circle of organizational relationships. Average leaders drew one of four patterns.

Twenty-five percent saw themselves as equals with customers and other team members, viewing themselves largely as nondirective facilitators who ultimately held no greater or lesser responsibility than others for results. We labeled these leaders *Bystanders* because they exert little influence over their environments and people around them, even though they perform their work dutifully within what they see as a "natural" structure. Their pictures looked like this:

The Bystander

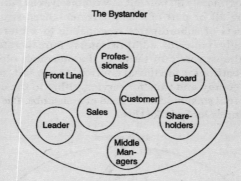

Nearly 20 percent of the control group saw themselves as what we call *Demigods*. They characterized themselves as dominant forces in their worlds, willing and able to do whatever it takes to control results, though primarily for their own benefit. These leaders exhibit a raw egocentricity based on the conviction that the force of their personality will save the day. However, since they typically fail to delegate and share with others, they seldom mobilize the support necessary to attain the highest levels of achievement. Their pictures looked like this:

The Demigod

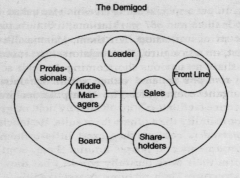

Approximately 30 percent saw themselves as *Bureaucrats*, overseeing all or part of a compartmentalized structure of distinct sets of subordinates responsible to a hierarchy of increasingly powerful administrators. Bureaucrats define success almost solely in terms of the outcomes of internal political battles for territorial control. As a result, they lack both the energy and time for service, either to the customer or to internal stakeholders in need of assistance. The Bureaucrats' pictures looked like this:

The Bureaucrat

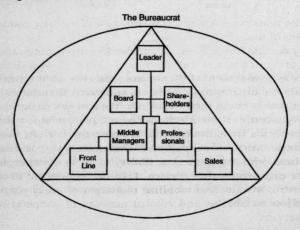

Finally, 16 percent saw themselves as *Manipulators,* who stood outside the circle of organizational life and attempted to pull the strings of others. For them, Machiavelli wasn't just a realist, he was a guru. Manipulators, Bureaucrats, and Demigods share an obvious shortcoming: In their schemes, the leader remains isolated either within or outside the circle of organizational life. The Manipulators drew this picture:

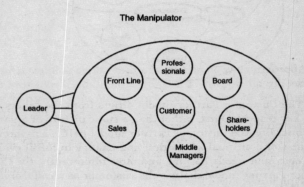

The Manipulator

The remaining 9 percent of average leaders drew combinations of these four scenarios.

By contrast, 96 percent of workleaders drew some variation of the *Customer Partner* model. They viewed themselves as advocates for the customer, traveling to the world outside the organization to escort and guide the customer to the center of organizational life. This model recognizes the organization's interdependence with the outside world and strikes a dynamic balance between the two. In their drawings, workleaders depicted themselves as customer advocates who assume responsibility to focus the energies of the organization on service. Like the conductor of an orchestra, workleaders mobilize the talent of every player to deliver a cohesive and vibrant message of cooperation and service.

The Customer Partner Model

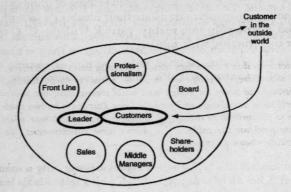

The Customer Partner model differs from the others in two key respects. First, rather than a static picture of organizational life, the Customer Partner model paints a dynamic process of continual adaptation and change to fulfill evolving customer needs. Second, and most importantly, the Customer Partner model defines the customer as a *collaborator in achievement*. Workleaders recognize that no one can control an organization solely from within. Real power lies in working with the external customers who invariably determine success or failure in the marketplace. The Customer Partner model pictures success as a function of shared achievement and, in turn, establishes a framework for relationships based on mutual empowerment and commitment.

➤ #5. Be Committed

I don't want "yes men" around me. I want everybody to tell me the truth . . . even if it costs them their jobs.

—SAMUEL GOLDWYN,
MGM mogul

Well, so much for commitment. Rejecting Sam Goldwyn's caustic view of life, workleaders build bridges of understanding and commitment to translate their ideals of a customer-focused partnership into reality. Patrick William, CEO of a major construction firm, told us:

> *I not only don't want "yes men," I literally can't afford them. If something's wrong, we need to know it immediately, because the more we design and build wrong now, the more we'll have to redesign and rebuild later. Our team knows that we're committed to them and, together, to the customer who puts food on the table. If we didn't have commitment, we wouldn't have a company.*

For leaders like William, work provides not only a means to an end, but an experience through which individuals learn to understand and commit to each other. They overcome the destructive behaviors of avoidance and contempt to connect with each other at ever increasing levels of involvement—proceeding from contact, awareness, involvement, empathy, and empowerment to commitment. Research by Salvatore Maddi and others has shown that, as a life force, commitment can overcome failure, anger, and personal loss. It instills patience and perseverance, and provides the key to developing resilience and hardiness in the face of adversity.

Our research revealed that commitment follows a ten-step process, moving from contempt and nonrelationship to commitment and strong bonds of partnership. It defines a ladder all leaders must climb to build a high-performance team. Through commitment, workleaders learn how to face and overcome adversity, building the optimism required to create a prosperous future with their associates.

➤ #6. Learn to Be an Optimist

Whatever can go wrong, will go wrong,
at the worst possible moment.

—THE OLD MURPHY'S LAW

Whatever should go right can go right,
on time and within budget.

—THE NEW MURPHY'S LAW

Since ancient times, the battle between optimism and pessimism—between the possibilities and limitations of the human condition—has raged without interruption. For workleaders, however, optimism has won the battle. To borrow a phrase from Martin Seligman, workleaders have become *learned optimists*. Recent psychological studies have shown not only that optimists enjoy greater success in life, but that optimism can be learned. Optimists, like exceptional leaders, are made and not born.

By applying their energies to self-improvement and achievement, workleaders have learned to face challenges head-on by relying on pragmatic problem-solving skills. Like Thomas Edison, workleaders use failure as a stepping stone to progress. When someone asked Edison if he had ever gotten discouraged during the thousand failed attempts to invent the light bulb, he replied: "No, I just learned how *not* to build a light bulb."

Workleaders learn how to transform even the most difficult situations into opportunities to serve and to build more committed relationships. In doing so, they counter naysayers and overcome disappointments. Learning how to cope with adversity and succeed despite the odds, they ultimately accept full responsibility for their lives, their customers' lives, and the lives of those who serve the customer.

➤ #7. Accept Responsibility

Toto, I have a feeling we're not in Kansas anymore.

—DOROTHY
in *The Wizard of Oz*

In their book, *The Oz Principle: Getting Results Through Individual and Organizational Accountability*, Roger Connors,

Tom Smith, and Craig Hickman use the story of Dorothy, the lion, the tin man, and the scarecrow to illustrate the fact that the things we most desire require us to assume personal responsibility. The four companions embark on a journey down the yellow brick road to get the results they want: transportation back to Kansas, courage, heart, and intelligence. After an arduous journey to see the wizard, they discover that they possessed the means to fulfill their dreams all along but couldn't apply those means until they accepted responsibility to do so for themselves.

To accept responsibility is to own your life, to fully commit to solving problems, to invest energy and imagination in self-improvement, to redress wrongs inflicted on others, and finally, like Dorothy, to face up to the reality of the situation at hand. Despite the occasional setback, workleaders have learned that personal achievement hinges on assuming responsibility for controlling one's personal destiny. Like the mythic circle of life, the seven principles of high Leadership IQ reveal an understanding of the way human progress evolves through a continuous loop of improvement—achievement begets pragmatism, humility, service to others, commitment, optimism, and the willingness to accept responsibility—qualities which, in turn, together reinforce the desire to achieve at ever-higher levels.

Workleaders take to heart the admonition, "Seize control of your destiny or someone else will." They know that control depends on mastering the Eight Workleader Roles and the tools they embody.

■ THE EIGHT WORKLEADER ROLES AND HIGH LEADERSHIP IQ

Our research led us to define eight distinct roles that workleaders fulfill in order to unlock the wisdom of the Seven Guiding Principles. These roles form an essential base of technical knowledge to accompany the liberal arts education of the Guiding Principles.

THE EIGHT WORKLEADER ROLES

Role 1: The Selector
   Purpose: Select for the customer.
   Tool #1: Focused Questioning
   Tool #2: Four Steps to Selection

Role 2: The Connector
   Purpose: Build and enhance relationships.
   Tool #1: The Connection Ladder
   Tool #2: The Relationship Styles Grid

Role 3: The Problem Solver
   Purpose: Produce results.
   Tool #1: The Problem Transformer
   Tool #2: The Problem Analysis and Solution Worksheet

Role 4: The Evaluator
   Purpose: Enhance individual performance.
   Tool #1: The Key Principles of Effective Evaluation
   Tool #2: The Performance Appraisal Worksheet

Role 5: The Negotiator
   Purpose: Serve the customer by achieving consensus on what needs to be done.
   Tool #1: The Customer Needs Analyzer
   Tool #2: The Consensus Negotiating Guide

Role 6: The Healer
   Purpose: Mend the fabric of organizational life.
   Tool #1: The Healing Needs Analyzer
   Tool #2: The Healing Guide

Role 7: The Protector
   Purpose: Diagnose and respond to threats to organizational well-being.
   Tool #1: The Risk Assessment Guide
   Tool #2: The Conflict Management Guide

Role 8: The Synergizer
   Purpose: Create a whole greater than the sum of its parts.
   Tool #1: Choices for Change
   Tool #2: The Seven-Step Guide to Self-Improvement

While the Eight Roles and their tools are informed by the Guiding Principles, developing the ability to carry out these roles can actually improve a workleader's knowledge of the Guiding Principles. (In fact, one intriguing finding of our research is that leaders who do not initially possess clear understanding of the Seven Guiding Principles quickly learn them as they master the Eight Roles.)

This fact emerged during a special substudy we performed to validate the assertion that leaders are made, not born, and that anyone can boost his or her Leadership IQ through study and practice. One hundred twenty-five average to low average performing leaders were selected to participate in the assessment and self-development process. As a result *all* improved their performance, and 73 joined the benchmark workleader group of 1,029 within 12 to 18 months.

These results highlight the importance of leadership development. In particular, both the research and the education demonstrate the importance of *scripts* as the principal medium of leadership action. Workleaders, it turns out, say just the right thing to just the right person at just the right time. For them, the transformation of knowledge into action results from a disciplined structure of dialogue. Like the Greek philosopher Socrates, superior leaders guide, teach, and direct through carefully conceived scripts that question, probe, challenge, and cajole. Through masterfully designed scripts, the workleaders in our study taught us how they transform abstract principles and values into daily actions in the real world of work.

■ A NEW MODEL FOR SUCCESS

Taken together, the Seven Guiding Principles and the Eight Workleader Roles that increase Leadership IQ provide a new model for success that virtually any leader in any organization can use with confidence.

Our research enabled us to define specific tools that help leaders succeed in each of the roles. In the following chapters we present two key tools for each role that will help you quickly improve your performance (see The Eight Workleader Roles chart).

■ THE SYNERGISTIC KICK

The new model of Leadership IQ integrates values, strategy, and practice, yet it is basically simple. Like the individual disciplines of the martial arts, the Seven Guiding Principles and Eight Workleader Roles bestow true benefit upon those who master them *all*. Only then can one achieve the synergistic kick.

The importance of mastering all the roles became clear when we weighed another major result of our study. Many of the less effective leaders we met exhibited very good to superior competency in several roles, yet their peers, subordinates, and supervisors rated their overall performance as merely adequate. While on the surface these individuals displayed 50 to 60 percent of the competency levels achieved by workleaders, they reached only 15 to 25 percent in terms of overall effectiveness. Why? The answer lies in the synergistic kick individuals achieve when they fulfill all of the roles, where each role interacts with and supports the others, just as the themes of a Beethoven symphony interconnect to create a masterpiece.

Workleaders turn in superior performances because they have learned how to harness the power of all the roles. Anyone can do the same. Entrepreneur or member of a Fortune 500 company, CEO or front-line worker, technical wizard or customer service representative—any leader can learn to work and lead more intelligently.

2

The Selector

One of the pivotal events in the battle against Nazi Germany was the selection of Dwight David Eisenhower to lead Operation OVERLORD, the major Allied offensive designed to deliver the final coup de grace to Hitler's campaign in Europe. By deciding to appoint Eisenhower, President Roosevelt and General George Marshall, Chief of Staff of the U.S. Armed Forces, changed the course of history.

George Marshall knew exactly what kind of person was needed and it wasn't any of his most senior officers. He dismissed the candidacies of such experienced commanders as General Douglas MacArthur, Field Marshall Bernard Montgomery, and General George Patton, feeling that all of these eminent and charismatic men were more interested in their careers than in the success of the mission.

Instead, Marshall needed someone driven by a higher motive, someone with the ability and strength to hold everyone accountable to the mission, someone both confident and humble enough to let others share the spotlight. "I knew that Eisenhower was the man," Marshall later said half-jokingly, "when I found out he was from Kansas."

By the time Marshall reached his decision, he knew a lot more about Eisenhower. They had shared lengthy discussions, and Marshall and FDR had carefully observed Eisenhower's conduct in various situations. When Marshall finally asked Eisenhower how he would accomplish the Allies' objective, Eisenhower explained that for anyone but such charismatic geniuses as MacArthur and Patton, the best route to success was *working through others*.

Hearing that, Marshall knew he had the right man. Eisenhower, on the other hand, wasn't quite as confident. He did accept the position, but only after more thought and discussion. He carefully and objectively analyzed the leadership needs of the European campaign and finally agreed to consider his own candidacy. With reservations that reflected his strategic humility, he came to agree that Marshall was right: In spite of his limitations, he could do the job. And, of course, he did the job brilliantly and later went on to serve two terms as President of the United States.

For Marshall and Eisenhower, a well-executed selection process led to one of the best selection decisions of the twentieth century. Each played an active role in the process: Marshall decided that Eisenhower was the right person for the job, and so did Eisenhower.

■ THE ROLE OF THE SELECTOR

Marshall and Eisenhower demonstrated the central goal of the selection process: Put the right person in the right place doing the right job at the right time. Selection is a pragmatic and collaborative process. Both the prospective employer and the prospective employee share the responsibility for making a wise decision. It is as unwise to take a job for which you are unsuited as it is to hire someone you know cannot succeed. Too often, people feel that the selection process is one-sided, and that the "more powerful" person is making all the decisions. Our research revealed that people with high Leadership IQ believe exactly the opposite: They see themselves as decision makers in all situations. Like Eisenhower, they are more concerned about making a choice themselves than whether someone else will offer them that choice. When asked to chronicle their growth and development, the exceptional leaders we studied consistently focused on the process of making an active selection as the pivotal event at every stage of their life histories. Even though they acknowledged the occasional relevance of luck, they invariably attributed their successes to their readiness to make choices. Being in the right place at the right time is important, but only for those ready to act on opportunities.

The following chart encapsulates what we have learned about the selection process. It can serve as a road map of the terrain you will explore in the pages ahead, where we discuss two tools for fulfilling the role of the selector, the technique of *Focused Questioning* and *Four Steps to Selection*. These tools were developed by studying the practices of the best leaders in our research group. In the following pages you will apply these tools to the four major activities of selection: hiring, reselection, debriefing, and separation.

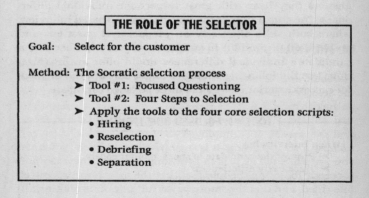

```
┌─────────────────────────────────────────────────────┐
│              THE ROLE OF THE SELECTOR                │
│                                                       │
│   Goal:     Select for the customer                  │
│                                                       │
│   Method:  The Socratic selection process            │
│            ➤ Tool #1:  Focused Questioning           │
│            ➤ Tool #2:  Four Steps to Selection       │
│            ➤ Apply the tools to the four core        │
│              selection scripts:                      │
│                • Hiring                               │
│                • Reselection                         │
│                • Debriefing                           │
│                • Separation                           │
│                                                       │
└─────────────────────────────────────────────────────┘
```

Like highly trained clinical diagnosticians, the best selectors know exactly what they are looking for in terms of experience, personality, and values when they interview a job candidate. All of their interview questions focus on the candidate's work history, including information related to education, training, and motivation. Work history, they explain, is the only thing that matters. "I believe fervently in equal opportunity," noted master selector Jill Lowenheim of the U.S. Department of Health and Human Services, "so I insist on using one standard upon which we can all agree—a person's achievement through work history." The goal in discussing work history and experience is to uncover people's values—in particular the values that determine their attitudes toward others, particularly customers. Leadership achievement begins and ends with the customer, so every decision must be considered in terms of its effect on the customer—whether the customer is an in-house employee or the general public.

➤ Tool #1: Focused Questioning

In a successful interview, high Leadership IQ people ask just the right questions at just the right time, and they weigh the answers they hear with great respect for individual differences. The constraints of the routine, resume-based interview, where both sides often rely on prepackaged questions and answers, often prohibit investigation of just what benefits a candidate's individual differences would offer an organization. Use the following strategies to get beneath the dressed-for-success exterior of even the most polished candidate.

TOOL #1: FOCUSED QUESTIONING

When interviewing
- ➤ Prompt the candidate to speak spontaneously.
- ➤ Track early experiences.
- ➤ Let the candidate do the talking.

When being interviewed
- ➤ Ask about the values of people who have been successful.
- ➤ Do independent research.
- ➤ Don't rely on your resume.

➤ *Prompt the candidate to speak spontaneously.* It is no surprise that if candidate Janet Doe knows the interviewer will ask about the eight-month gap in her employment history, she will fabricate and rehearse the response she thinks the interviewer wants to hear. But if the interviewer asks her to describe her most rewarding experience during that hiatus, she may reveal something crucial about herself and her values. High achievers conduct fruitful interviews by knowing how to work around the traditional interview script.

➤ *Ask about the candidate's earliest experiences in the workforce.* Candidates give a lot of thought to the ways their recent professional experience gives them an edge in their field. Skilled selectors have learned to ask about formative work histories—the experiences a candidate may not realize are related to the job at hand and any job. Janet Doe's thoughts about her teen years as a line cook at a fast food restaurant will shed light on her potential performance as vice president of marketing.

➤ *Let the candidate do most of the talking.* A good conversationalist is really a good listener. The bulk of the talking in nearly any interview (except for the separation interview) is done by the candidate. Rather than force the person you're interviewing to read for cues and respond with what he or she guesses is the "correct" response, accomplished selectors steer the direction of the conversation, but let the interviewee do most of the talking.

There is an art to being interviewed as well. The goal of the job candidate is to learn as much about the company and the interviewer as possible. The following strategies help workleaders look beyond the facades of glossy annual reports and carefully crafted press releases to uncover the truth about any organization.

➤ *Ask what specific qualities are shared by people who are successful in the organization.*

➤ *Do independent research.* The interviewer will try to keep you talking. And whatever the interviewer tells you about the company and your potential position has been as well prepared as most annual reports. Do your *own* research on potential workplaces as carefully as possible, and be sure to ask questions.

➤ *Don't rely on your resume.* Your resume can't convey all that you have to offer an organization. You have to communicate it to the interviewer in person as well.

TOOL #2: FOUR STEPS TO SELECTION

For Hiring, Reselection, Debriefing

Step 1: Establish a context for action.
- ➤ Be nonthreatening.
- ➤ Set a private and courteous tone.
- ➤ Prevent interruptions.

Step 2: Conduct a formal assessment.
- ➤ Ask primary questions—assess work history.
- ➤ Ask probing questions—assess transitions.

Step 3: Diagnose and evaluate results.
- ➤ Clarify information.
- ➤ Follow up information.
- ➤ Assess "goodness of fit" of the candidate.

Step 4: Take action.
- ➤ Reinforce or reject the decision.
- ➤ Inform all candidates of the decision.

For Separation

Step 1: Conduct a formal assessment.

Step 2: Diagnose and evaluate results.
- ➤ Consider the decision carefully.

Step 3: Establish a formal context.
- ➤ State the decision up front.
- ➤ Calmly review the basis for the decision.

Step 4: Take action.
- ➤ Does the person understand?
- ➤ Does he or she have questions?
- ➤ Repeat the conclusion.
- ➤ Provide information regarding arrangements.

➤ Tool #2: Four Steps to Selection

The selection process comprises four basic steps:

1. Establish an appropriate atmosphere.
2. Conduct a formal assessment.
3. Diagnose and evaluate the results.
4. Take action.

These steps remain constant whether you are hiring a new candidate, evaluating someone for promotion or a shift in responsibilities, or conducting an exit interview. Selection scripts concentrate on gathering information. They follow the pattern of a Socratic dialogue—each party strives to elicit just the right information by asking just the right questions. As the Talmudic scholar replied when asked why he answered every question with another question, "So what's wrong with a question?" According to the rules of Socratic dialogue, the person asking the questions guides the conversation toward a desired goal by encouraging detailed, directed answers. However, in all cases but the separation interview where the selector does 80 percent of the talking, the interviewer should spend 65 to 75 percent of the conversation listening to the answers. As the old admonition advises, "God gave us two ears and one mouth for a reason."

Step 1: Establish a Context for Action

A key element in this step involves setting the proper tone for the conversation: relaxed, personal, respectful, and civil. Like John Gritmon, an information systems executive at Coors, high Leadership IQ people never forget that they are speaking *with* people, not *at* them. A nonconfrontational and nonhierarchical setting helps. To establish rapport, the setting should communicate your interest, not your power. For example, sitting across the desk from a candidate indicates that you perceive yourself as the boss; this can make people nervous and defensive. Simply moving from behind a desk to sit beside someone, or meeting in an informal setting such as a conference room with some refreshments handy, can set the proper collegial, rather than adversarial, tone for the meeting.

Step 2: Conduct a Formal Assessment

After opening pleasantries, get right to the heart of the conversation and address the person's work history. The adept interviewer approaches this subject directly but always displays respect and courtesy. This approach enables an interviewer to ask ever more penetrating questions that delve into the real person behind the packaged resume (or the real company behind the glossy annual report). The transition points in candidates' work histories reveal the most about their judgment. Like a musical performance that glides effortlessly from one key and section to another, the modulations and bridges in a life history reveal a lot about the quality of a performer. How well did the candidate handle those crucial transitions?

Step 3: Diagnose and Evaluate Results

This step begins with summary observations designed to clarify and review key points. At the close of the meeting, the selector paraphrases what he or she has heard and asks the candidate to supplement the information or correct any inaccurate interpretations. After concluding the meeting, the selector evaluates the potential fit between the needs and qualities of the candidate and the organization, while the candidate does the same. This phase may include reference checks by both parties and follow-up discussions as needed. In any event, potential partners avoid hasty decisions. A little extra time spent examining information from all angles will pay off in the long run. The amount of information generated by a work history review is far greater than people are used to receiving, and takes some time to digest.

Step 4: Take Action

At this stage the interviewer promptly and incisively communicates the decision and the reasoning for it. Values and principles come into play as the context of the selection is reinforced. In a well-performed selection process, as the interviewer explains the decision it becomes apparent to the interviewee that values of partnership and service have been affirmed through the principles of Socratic questioning and empathy.

➤ A Script for Hiring — Paul's Story

We met Paul shortly after he had gone through the selection process himself; he had been chosen by the board of directors of Teledynamics to turn around a rather desperate financial situation. "I came to Teledynamics," he told us, "because I really believed that the people there wanted to create a special company. Somewhere along the line, though, the dream of great financial rewards got disconnected from a true commitment to service. As a result, they were bleeding red ink."

Paul brought a clear set of values to his new job. "Success in business these days is all about the battle for democracy, providing greater access to ideas and information through better service. *To win the battle, people in the front lines of service must have access to other people's knowledge. In other words, we also have to serve those who serve. Putting the right people in the right place to do it is the key to success in this industry.*"

This bedrock belief prompted Paul to institute a selection and reselection process throughout Teledynamics following the principles of Socratic questioning and empathy. "It started with the board selecting me and me selecting the company. Now, I had to hire a chief operating officer in a way that demonstrated my commitment to my belief and my principles."

Paul explained how he began: "We used a search firm to find candidates—high achievers, that's what I insisted on. Well, one of them was a former Secret Service agent named Bruce whose resume of accomplishments suggested a great fit. He passed through all the other screening interviews with flying colors, so I asked to meet with him personally."

Paul said that one of the tip-offs that Bruce's sterling resume concealed a potentially damaging weakness emerged when he asked Bruce to discuss his work history. "I asked Bruce about his early work experiences," Paul told us. "But he kept turning the conversation to his recent successes, and the high points on his resume." Paul told us that at this point he made a tactical decision to back off from his own agenda and allow Bruce to guide the interview. "I just sat back and waited to see where this would lead us. Bruce started talking about his recent series of promotions, his MBA from Michigan, and then what he called the rigorous selection process he went through to get into the Secret Service. So I asked him to tell me more about that selection process."

As Paul related it to us, the conversation went as follows.

Step 1: Establishing a Context

Paul wanted to conduct the interview in an informal atmosphere, partly to convey his beliefs about the importance of teamwork and partly as an effort to put the candidate at ease because, as he told us, "It's hard to do a good interview with nervous people." For the following exchange, Paul and Bruce sat side by side at a conference table at Teledynamics. Paul first offered Bruce coffee, which Bruce accepted but never touched. Paul also took coffee and occasionally sipped it.

Step 2: Conducting the Formal Assessment

Bruce: *(In response to Paul's question about the selection process for the Secret Service.)* Well, to be honest, Paul, it was nothing like this. It was very demanding. I had to perform before a three-man panel who hit me with a bunch of very difficult questions.

Paul: Such as?

Bruce: Well, they were very conceptual and insightful, I thought. Did I believe in the principles of the constitution? Was I capable of handling stressful situations? Did I have trouble responding to authority? Did I have the intelligence and courage to do what was necessary? Those types of questions.

Paul told us, "Bruce seemed to relax a bit while he was talking about his time in the Secret Service. He was obviously very proud of his experiences there. And since he seemed more comfortable, I told him his story was interesting, and asked what led him to the Secret Service, and what he did before that. This led me back to my original questions about Bruce's early work history. He told me his first work experience was at his uncle's tailor shop."

Paul: What did you learn in that experience, at your uncle's tailor shop?

Bruce: *(Speaking as though this is a matter about which he has thought often and has definite feelings.)* It gave me ambition.

Paul: Well can you tell me about that? What do you mean?

Bruce: At the shop you had no control over your life: You were constantly at the beck and call of others. Customers can be very demanding—which is generally well within their rights—but anyway, we had to work very hard. Six days a week. From very early in the morning—we started working at around 6:30 A.M.—to sometimes late at night. And when there were special orders, we'd be open on Sundays, too. In that kind of situation you're just not in control of your life.

Paul: Can you give me an example of what you mean?

Bruce: Well, for example, once when I was a kid, about sixteen I think, someone came in to get a suit we'd tailored. I remember I gave it to him and he thought something was wrong with it and he got very upset. He called me irresponsible, and told me that we didn't know what we were doing. He said, "You people just can't be trusted with anything." And he went on. I decided after that that I didn't have to take this kind of treatment. And I wondered why my uncle was taking it. I figured he had to, that he got trapped. So I determined I wasn't going to be in that situation. I wasn't going to take anyone's orders that way. That's what I mean by ambition.

Paul explained: "It was an emotional story. I wanted to hear more, but I tried to shift the conversation—to give Bruce a chance to stop being so emotional about the situation. That way he could tell me more clearly about his conception of ambition. I still wasn't sure what he meant, or how this could affect his work."

Paul: Were you the only one who worked in the shop? Were there any other young people employed there, like you?

Bruce: My cousin also worked there.

Paul: So your cousin was a co-worker at the tailor shop? What was that like, working with your cousin as a colleague?

"I asked it that way," Paul said, "because while I wanted to know the answer, I knew I couldn't ask about his personal relationships. It seemed fair to ask about his cousin as a colleague, but not just about his cousin."

Bruce: He got out of there too. He's an ophthalmological surgeon. He's been very successful.

Paul: Well, what other lessons did you learn from working in your uncle's shop?

Bruce: I learned that you can't be respected by most people for that kind of work. You end up a prisoner in a one-sided relationship.

Paul: What kind of a relationship do you want to work with?

Bruce: A relationship in which standards of success are recognized.

Paul: (Puzzled.) Do you think that in most relationships they're not?

Bruce: Well, we want to work as teammates and as colleagues, but someone has to be recognized as an authority in a situation.

Paul: What does that mean in practice? How do *you* confront problems, and how do you work with people?

Bruce: I make sure they understand what their job is, what their responsibility is, and that they accept this responsibility. I make it clear that I expect results and that people show respect for the system.

Paul: *(Rephrasing.)* Does that mean that you feel it's important that people understand that you're the boss?

Bruce: Yes, if I'm the boss. Or someone else if they're the boss. I think it's important that people understand lines of authority and who's who in the chain of command. You really can't get anything done if people don't understand who's in charge.

Paul: I see. And if you were to characterize yourself as a leader, how would you describe yourself?

Bruce: Well, I'm a direct, forceful leader who insists that the best kind of work be produced and who insists that people take responsibility for their work. I think people might say that I'm a bit hard-nosed, but fair.

Paul: *(Making a conjecture, and asking to make sure that it's accurate.)* Would people also describe you as a person who is in charge and makes it clear to others that they are responsible to him to get that job done?

"His answer to that," said Paul, "was 'Yes.'"

Step 3: Paul's Diagnosis and Evaluation of the Results

"My concern about Bruce was that we were building a team of colleagues, and that at any given time, the worker could be the boss, and the boss could be the worker," Paul explained. "I thought Bruce would have difficulty understanding that concept. He seemed to see advancement as a way of becoming more and more fully in charge, not as a way of becoming a colleague. I admired Bruce's accomplishments. His background, knowledge and credentials were very good. My decision hinged on his perception of what leadership was about."

It was by looking beyond Bruce's resume that Paul found the most valuable information about Bruce's perspectives on service and leadership. Paul believed that Bruce would be an ambitious, almost predatory executive who would find it difficult to respect his colleagues and other shareholders in his sphere of influence. Bruce lacked an understanding of the larger context in which he worked: He did not see success as corporate maturity, or as increased responsibility, but as power. Paul decided not to offer Bruce the job. He kept his values at the center of the selection process, and when it became clear that Bruce did not embrace those values—respect for every partner as a valuable contributor and a commitment to serving the customer—Paul knew that Bruce would not fit the job at Teledynamics. As Paul told us, "In the twenty-first century business environment the workforce is diverse, the customer body is diverse, and information and knowledge are key. In a world where at any given time a secretary might have more information than the CEO, Bruce would definitely be uncomfortable, and he'd probably be a liability."

Step 4: Taking Action

Although he decided not to hire Bruce, Paul soon concluded his search, selecting (and being selected by) Janice Czech, an internal candidate whose steady progression through the industry during a 20-year career had earned her the consistent admiration of her peers, supervisors, and subordinates. When Paul described the difference between the meetings with Bruce and Janice, he called the former a monologue and the latter a dialogue, concluding that, "Before my meeting with Janice was over, not only had we thoroughly covered her work history, we had dissected this company as well. We were already deep into problem solving an hour into it. You know, it's funny, but the difference between the two candidates came down to one word. Bruce must have said 'I' fifty times. Janice always said 'we.' She had *service to the customer* written all over her."

Paul's story taught us a lot about the practices of workleaders. Some of the key points we found are:

➤ *Define your principles before conducting interviews.* Paul was greatly aided in the decision process because he already knew that his choice would be guided by his belief in the importance of information sharing. While an independent or charismatic leader might sometimes be a suitable choice, Paul's situation and principles demanded a team player.

➤ Don't *limit your questions to items covered in the resume.* This is common sense, but we found that it certainly *isn't* common practice with most interviewers.

➤ *Evaluate the candidate's readiness for questions.* Bruce was more willing to discuss his early work experiences after he had communicated what he felt were his high points.

➤ *Try to fully understand what the candidate is telling you.* Paul showed his commitment to the selection process by pressing Bruce to explain ambiguous terms and ideas.

➤ *Ask the candidate what his or her principles or character would mean in actual practice.* Paul asked Bruce to characterize his ideas of work relationships and leadership.

➤ A Script for Reselection—Alethea's Story

Our study also showed that the most successful leaders develop the ability to carefully evaluate and reevaluate existing team members in order to distribute responsibilities and rewards in the most effective manner possible. They know that people grow and change and that effective leadership requires a clear understanding of that growth and change. The reselection script provides an ideal vehicle for making such evaluations. Alethea Freeman, vice president of sales for Adams, Inc., a multistate home appliances company, used the following reselection script to deal with an emotionally sensitive and potentially draining situation.

Just days after Alethea Freeman won her promotion to vice president of sales for Adams, she initiated a reselection conversation with Jesse Adams, one of the company's most respected and experienced salespeople. Jesse's performance had taken a nosedive, and Alethea needed to find out what had caused his rather sudden decline in productivity.

Step 1: Establishing a Context

To establish the right setting for the conversation, Alethea invited Jesse to lunch at a casual restaurant far enough away from the office to not run into any co-workers. She began the meeting by reinforcing Jesse's self-esteem, expressing her admiration for his outstanding record of dedication and service. At the same time, she carefully but officially turned the discussion toward his surprising drop-off in productivity, a concern she felt sure he shared.

Step 2: Conducting the Formal Assessment:

Alethea: You have an excellent record, which makes your recent sales figures all the more striking. Would you mind, though, if we set that issue aside for a moment and talked about a more basic question—namely, you? Who is Jesse

Adams? What does he think of his job, his customers and the Adams family?

As Alethea told us: "Despite his obvious discomfort, Jesse agreed. In fact, he seemed relieved at the chance to get something off his chest."

Jesse: I'm not sure where to begin.

Alethea: I'm new at this, too, so we'll have to play it by ear. But I'd like to suggest that we start at the beginning. Does that make sense?

Jesse: Yeah. I've had some great years here.

Alethea explained to us: "To be honest, I'd decided to use that script long before we sat down to talk. Since Adams was his family's business, I wondered about Jesse's motives for going into it. I didn't know if he just needed some time to recharge, or if he felt burned out after years of obligatory service, or what. Still, of course, I had to make sure that Jesse felt comfortable going all the way back to Act I of his career at Adams."

Alethea continued the assessment phase by asking Jesse to walk her through his work history, beginning with his first job. As Alethea reconstructed the conversation, "Jesse said, 'Sure,' and began telling me that he joined the company in 1954 as a stock boy. Here I interrupted and asked him if that was really his first job. He said, 'No,' and told me about a job he had in 1950. Was that the very first one? Again he shook his head and told me about something in 1947. That's the first one? No, again. Finally, he chuckled and said, 'Look Alethea, I've never told anyone this but my first job was in 1937, when I was six years old.' And he went on to explain that he is the oldest of four kids and they'd lost their parents in a car accident that year. They were split up and lived with relatives. Jesse lived on an aunt's farm and worked every day. 'I saved enough money to buy each of my brothers and sisters a Christmas gift that first year,' he said, 'and, from then on, I became the parent.' "

Once the floodgates opened, Jesse poured out a work history that spanned more than five decades of steady, uninterrupted employment. As he talked, Alethea began to see that Jesse viewed his life as a continuum of service to two sets of families: first to his brothers and sisters and, second, to his own children. Jesse had dropped out of high school to work full time at Adams, his grandfather's business, and from then on he had moved steadily up the ladder, climbing from stock boy to vice president of operations. When that position disappeared after a merger four years ago, he crossed over into sales. His sales record followed the same upward curve as the rest of his work history. Jesse spoke with pride and satisfaction about his long career and the accomplishments of "both sets of children" and of his wife, a recently retired teacher. Through Jesse's tale emerged a multifaceted person who had hesitated to talk about his many talents and accomplishments for fear that his lack of formal education might turn off his new boss. Alethea assured Jesse otherwise, took a deep breath, and asked Jesse the hard question: "How did you feel while you were driving to this meeting?"

Step 3: Alethea and Jesse's Diagnosis and Evaluation of the Results

"I knew I might strike a nerve with that one," Alethea told us. "I was trying to gauge just how burned out he was. Jesse had been working nonstop for 58 years, and I guessed that might explain his recent setback. I was right. He sighed, looked me straight in the eyes, and said 'I just felt tired.' "

Alethea: You didn't feel nervous?

Jesse: Nope. Nothing makes me nervous anymore. I've seen it all here at Adams.

> *Alethea:* (Using a question to emphasize Jesse's ultimate responsibility for his own job satisfaction.) So. What can we do about your feeling tired?
>
> *Jesse:* I need a new job.

This took Alethea by surprise, but the more she thought about it, the more it made perfect sense. This man had immersed his life in service, so what better way to reenergize his zest for life than a job that would put his values back to work? Certainly not retirement, though Jesse qualified for it.

> *Alethea:* (Again, emphasizing Jesse's autonomy in this matter.) Did you have a dream job in mind?
>
> *Jesse:* I realize my performance has been lousy lately, but there must be a way for Adams to benefit from my experience and knowledge.
>
> *Alethea:* Do you want to get off the road?
>
> *Jesse:* More than half of what I do is customer relations. Isn't there a desk job where I could do that? Maybe I could help the new kids get the hang of it.

Alethea told Jesse she'd consider his idea, then ended their conversation by asking him to meet with her again in two days. As he left, she reached out her hand to Jesse and expressed her genuine admiration, telling him she had learned a lot from meeting him.

Step 4: Taking Action

Alethea thought long and hard about Jesse over the next two days. After consulting with Adams' human resources department she decided to offer Jesse a reassignment to a position that added a training component to an inside sales job. She laughed when she told us this: "Really, we *created* that job for Jesse. He was a company figurehead—it wasn't just that he was an Adams, he'd been a leading salesman for a long time and part of the company for over half a century. He's a sign of stability in a work world where people don't even seem to look for job security any more. And taking this into account plus his proven sales ability, who better to mentor the new hires? While he seemed to have passed his sales peak— though I thought that the reassignment might even help him out in this area—Jesse was too valuable to let go."

Jesse agreed to a tradeoff for the new job. With his cooperation and some careful planning that took into consideration his retirement benefits, Jesse took a 40 percent cut in salary and happily jumped into the new assignment. He and the company benefited from the assignment, as did both external and internal customers, including people who bought appliances from Adams and the new recruits who learned a lot from Jesse about the company's values.

Alethea's story illustrates the power of reselection as a strategy for change. Recognizing her need to know more about Jesse before deciding on a course of action to remedy a performance problem, Alethea initiated a leadership intervention that caused a rippling effect of positive results. Some of her successful strategies were:

➤ *Meet with a colleague rather than 'call him or her in' to express concerns.* The restaurant was a neutral and informal meeting place. Alethea explained to us that she did not want the meeting to take place in a threatening atmosphere: "I'm sure Jesse could guess that we were meeting to discuss his poor performance. I thought that by asking him to come to the restaurant I could convey to him that I wasn't calling him in to dress him down—or fire him."

➤ *Engage the colleague in his or her own survival.* Alethea reached out to Jesse with the same empathy and commitment to service she applies to her customers.

➤ *Address the issue head-on.* Rather than allowing tension to build, Alethea tactfully came to her point early on in the conversation. Jesse's relief was apparent.

➤ *Consider all parties involved in the situation.* In addressing the problem of Jesse's sagging sales, Alethea protected the rights of the customer and the capacity of the company to provide service. She sent a message to everyone in the company about the importance of continually reselecting their roles in work and life; she also showed the organization's commitment to all of its shareholders by becoming involved in Jesse's situation and by seeing how his presence could benefit new salespeople.

Had the situation been different, Jesse might have chosen to exit the firm altogether. In that case, Alethea would have used a debriefing script much like Don Walsh's, which follows.

➤ **A Script for Debriefing—Don's Story**

Another important application of the selection script is debriefing people who choose to leave of their own accord or due to an organizational restructuring that has nothing to do with their performance. The debriefing conversation goes far beyond the typical separation interview which generally deals only with the mechanics of the dismissal and tries to effect an amicable parting. Debriefing involves a reality assessment for both parties to compare an individual's developmental path and skills with the organization's current service and survival needs. If a good fit once existed, what factors have made a separation necessary? During our study workleaders adamantly expressed their need to fully understand what went wrong on *both* sides of the employment equation. They approach the situation as an opportunity to learn something valuable from someone with little to lose by being honest. Don Walsh, a vice president for IBM, explained the importance of this approach and how it works.

"To say the least," Don observed, "we've had a lot to learn during the past few years. And some of the most important lessons we've learned have come from people who have either had to leave us due to our restructuring or who chose other opportunities. While you might think these meetings would be intensely stressful, they're usually not. People want to help each other and, in the process, themselves, by understanding how a new reality emerged.

"We always begin those meetings by asking associates if they would mind reviewing their work history both before and during their time with us. In the midst of all the change we've faced, it's critically important to make sure we understand what's happened when and why."

Don added, "This was brought home by an interview I had with one of our exiting production line workers, Louise Poplowski, who had been recruited from Texas Instruments ten years ago to head a production work redesign team. Her personal development history paralleled every stage of our systems development, including the dramatic redesign in our production process that led to the elimination of her position. Her ability to articulate the strengths and weaknesses of each stage provided invaluable insight, however, and I thought her analytical skills were too good to lose. I therefore asked her to participate in a meeting with our new Group Manager, who retained Louise as a consultant after she left, with no hard feelings, I might add."

Don's story illustrates the value of the debriefing script, which follows the four basic steps of any situation script. Rather than walk through the account of his interview with Louise, Don gave us the following tips:

➤ *Let the interviewee know immediately that this is a separation interview, not a reselection interview.* Establish this fact firmly for yourself before starting the interview, and don't waver from your decision.

➤ *Be clear that the separation does not reflect negatively on the interviewee's contribution to the organization.* Refer the interviewee to the internal resources that are available.

➤ *Talk about the interviewee's work experience for the organization in terms that allow him or her to feel a sense of closure.* Help the interviewee see that work experience as a series of accomplishments, not just as a certain period of time—which is now ended—doing an activity.

Again, for debriefing, use a script that focuses on the organization's continued commitment to values, principles, and action, and emphasize the decision's consistency with that commitment. A win–win situation can be established by focusing on an individual's developmental history and the special insights he or she has gained at each stage—these same insights give the organization knowledge about itself as well.

Workleaders also operate with a goal of upholding the organizational mission when they must terminate a person's employment, though they use a much modified script to do so.

➤ A Script for Separation—Alice's Story

Termination of employment poses perhaps the most difficult challenge any workleader will face. Informing an associate that the organization no longer needs his or her services requires more careful preparation than the other selection scripts. Otherwise, the conversation can become painful and even destructive.

Unlike the other types of selection, in this situation the interviewer does most of the talking. The conversation should also take place in a more formal context. At the very outset, the leader should state clearly and forthrightly that a decision has been made to dismiss the person. Then the leader should calmly and thoroughly review the reasons behind the decision, emphasizing that it is final and irrevocable.

Alice Derry, an adept workleader who owns Derry Accounting Services, gave us valuable insights into the separation interview. She explained, "There is an old saying that if you don't lop off from the bottom, you'll lose from the top. We have an obligation to our customers both within and outside our company to provide top-quality service. If someone is just unable or unwilling to do what the job requires, then separation is in order. We undertake selection very carefully, and we're serious about evaluation and counseling if necessary. So if those processes haven't helped, it's time to move on. And if we don't, I've learned that our top performers will move on. They're the ones who lose the most when you fail to maintain a clean house."

The interview includes Steps 1 and 4, establishing a context and taking definitive action. It is necessary to conduct a formal assessment and diagnose and evaluate its results carefully (Steps 2 and 3) *before* deciding upon separation.

Step 1: Set the Context

Alice explained that while the separation conversation requires empathy and should allow for some discussion, the leader should assert control by focusing on the single purpose that has brought the parties together. The meeting should be as brief as possible, and it should minimize discussion of details regarding timing, severance pay, and outplacement—topics that can appropriately be handled later by someone with detailed technical knowledge. Alice prepares a written script that helps keep her on track if the situation becomes stressful. Before the interview, Alice takes 10 to 20 minutes to settle herself into a calm and collected frame of mind. Then she asks the subject in and directs him or her to take a seat across the desk from her.

Step 4: Take Action

Because Steps 2 and 3 must be completed *before* Alice takes action to terminate employment, she moves straight from Step 1 to Step 4 in the actual separation interview. Here Alice straightforwardly tells the person that she has convened the meeting to discuss an immediate separation. She doesn't get bogged down in lengthy issues that could sidetrack the basic conversation from its intended goal. And she avoids offering recommendations to future employers except in the case of a termination due to restructuring, in which case she stresses outplacement services.

Alice suggests that if the person wants to ask a lot of questions about the decision, the interviewer should say, "We're here to discuss our separation, not the evaluation, counseling, disciplinary, and problem-solving efforts that we've already been through. It's time for all of us to move on."

Alice also cites her major concern during the termination interview: "To implement the decision as cleanly and firmly as possible. My energies and the other person's need to be put into addressing the realities of the present and the immediate future. It's time to move on, leave the negative behind and regain positive momentum."

Alice's strategy, like that of other workleaders, reveals carefully crafted thinking. She recognizes the importance and difficulty of the situation and thoroughly prepares herself for it.

Alice gave us the following tips:

➤ *Hold separation meetings face-to-face across a desk.* A conversational side-by-side setting is not appropriate in this situation.

➤ *Try to restrict the conversation to 10 minutes.* Ted Lowe, former Chair of Languages at Holy Cross College and president of an international translating services company, agreed with Alice on this. He said, "I've invested enough energy, and so have others. If you have to break a leg, it's better to do it swiftly."

➤ *In general, try to schedule the termination meeting at the end of the day, preferably at the end of the week.* This decreases the potential for negative interactions with other staff immediately after the meeting. It also allows the dismissed person to save face and begin grieving in private.

➤ *Send positive signals to all employees that the decision will benefit the organization.* Any separation affects everyone in the organization. Through their track records, workleaders demonstrate to their organizations' stakeholders that their actions are consistent with the organizational mission.

The termination script does differ markedly from other scripts. However, it is similar in one crucial aspect: It centers on values. In cases of separation the dismissed individual has shown that his or her values, performance, or commitment have diverged from those of the organization. Workleaders make it crystal clear to the individual and to stakeholders that any option but separation would undermine team members' contributions and would be detrimental to customer service. Workleaders handle separation swiftly and surely. Since they invest the vast majority of their time on positive, proactive activities, they wish to get past such a negative event as quickly as possible.

■ FULFILLING THE ROLE OF THE SELECTOR

The workleaders we met during our study agree that life and work are matters of choice, and making the right choices depends on forming deep-seated values and developing principles based on those values—principles capable of shaping decisions. Whether hiring or being hired, reselecting, debriefing, or separating, workleaders keep their values at the heart of their decisions.

We learned from our study that the selection processes must be mastered first. Without it, the other disciplines of achievement—connection, problem solving, evaluation, negotiation, healing, protection, and synergy—cannot come into play. Having made the right choices, workleaders turn their attention to fostering the connections which permit individuals to work as a team.

3

The Connector

It is hard to imagine a person more isolated from the world than a six-year-old child who has not seen a ray of light, heard a sound, or uttered a word for nearly her whole life. It is even harder to imagine how a 21-year-old teacher could not only reveal the world to that child, but could eventually draw her so thoroughly into it that she would become a world-famous lecturer and writer. The remarkable story of that child, Helen Keller, and her teacher, Annie Sullivan, not only symbolizes the art of connection, but beautifully illustrates the way commitment can engender connection.

Helen Keller was born in 1880 in Tuscumbia, Alabama, into very comfortable circumstances, but a year and a half later an attack of scarlet fever deprived her completely of her senses of sight, hearing, and smell. She lived in darkness and silence for nearly five years until Annie Sullivan entered her life.

Knowing that she needed to find a pathway directly into Helen's world, Annie convinced Helen's parents to let her work alone with the child in a little house on their property. She spent grueling hours there with Helen, attempting to find physical and intellectual ways to unlock the door to her isolation. On April 15, 1887, as Helen held a mug under the well spout and water overflowed the mug onto one of Helen's hands, Annie spelled w-a-t-e-r into the other hand. Helen responded by reaching for Annie's hand and begging for new words. The breakthrough had occurred.

Annie Sullivan built a connection. She reached Helen across the silent darkness of her physical hardship and emotional alienation. Thus began a lifelong partnership of learning and growth that resulted in Helen Keller's transformation from a "wild animal" into a graduate of Radcliffe College, a member of the Massachusetts Commission for the Blind, a popular lecturer on the possibilities of intellectual life for the deaf and blind, and the author of half a dozen books.

■ THE ROLE OF THE CONNECTOR

Annie Sullivan's accomplishment was driven by her profound desire to connect. Nothing could alter her commitment. She tried—over and over again. Eventually, she succeeded.

This extraordinary level of commitment is as characteristic of people with high Leadership IQ as it is of Annie Sullivan. Leaders cannot do their work without the bridges of hope and optimism that enable them to join forces with others to create a new and better world. Like Annie Sullivan, the individuals in our study never let even seemingly insurmountable obstacles to connection get in their way. Work-leaders don't wait for others to reach out to them. Rather,

---

THE ROLE OF THE CONNECTOR

Goal: Build and enhance relationships

Method: Multipath communication
- ➤ Diagnose levels of connection/disconnection in key relationships with Tool #1: The Connection Ladder.
- ➤ Clarify communication needs with Tool #2: The Relationship Styles Grid.
- ➤ Customize communications to match preferred styles of relating.
- ➤ Transform the negative energy of opposition and contempt into the positive energy of commitment.
- ➤ Multipath with *all* stakeholders.

they assume the responsibility to connect. They don't expect others to tune into them—they tune into others.

Multipath or *M-pathic communication* is our name for this highly empathic method of connecting. Two tools will help you improve your ability to connect: the *Connection Ladder* and the *Relationship Styles Grid*. Both of these analytic tools will help you achieve a deeper understanding of those around you. Before we examine these tools more closely, consider the following comprehensive picture of the process of connection.

➤ Tool #1: The Connection Ladder

Average leaders tend to jump into relationships and try to implement communication strategies *without* assessing their audiences' receptibility or communication aptitudes. The best leaders *always* assess an audience before designing a strategy. The Connection Ladder provides a handy tool for such an assessment:

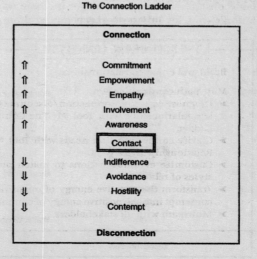

The Connection Ladder

	Connection
⇑	Commitment
⇑	Empowerment
⇑	Empathy
⇑	Involvement
⇑	Awareness
	Contact
⇓	Indifference
⇓	Avoidance
⇓	Hostility
⇓	Contempt
	Disconnection

Bill Johnson, a team leader who needed four team members to commit meaningfully to a six-month project, found himself dealing with four very different people who displayed varying levels of commitment. Susan Todd reacted rather passively to the challenge, expressing no strong opinion about how it should be accomplished and giving the impression, with a shrug of her shoulders, that she really couldn't care less about it. Bill labeled her as *indifferent*. Frank DeLucci, on the other hand, responded enthusiastically to the assignment, immediately offering ideas on how to get the job done, affirming his belief that the team possessed the skills to do an excellent job, and encouraging everyone to dig into it. Bill positioned him as *empowered*.

The third member, Joan Fox, expressed mild enthusiasm for the task, supporting Frank's point of view and clearly willing to follow his lead. To Bill, she seemed *aware*. Walter Bingham, on the other hand, voiced anger that Bill expected the team to create a report in what he viewed as an unreasonable amount of time, confiding that he never wanted to be on this team in the first place. Bill quickly placed Walter on the *contempt* rung of the ladder.

The Connection Ladder

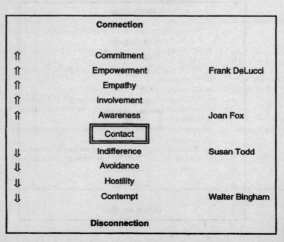

	Connection	
⇑	Commitment	
⇑	Empowerment	Frank DeLucci
⇑	Empathy	
⇑	Involvement	
⇑	Awareness	Joan Fox
	Contact	
⇓	Indifference	Susan Todd
⇓	Avoidance	
⇓	Hostility	
⇓	Contempt	Walter Bingham
	Disconnection	

Bill Johnson used the Connection Ladder to assess his team members' levels of commitment. The following chart details the behaviors he looked for when he assessed each person's position on the ladder. It can help you do the same.

THE CONNECTION LADDER	

CONNECTION		
⇑	Commitment	Meaningful relationship
		➤ High level of mutual understanding and trust
		➤ Significant personal bonding
		➤ Effective collaborative effort
⇑	Empowerment	Sharing of control
		➤ Giving and receiving information; providing options
		➤ Reinforcing the other person's inner strengths and resources
		➤ Encouraging the other person to take on as much responsibility as is reasonably possible
⇑	Empathy	Emotional nurturing
		➤ Walking in the other person's shoes without putting them on
		➤ Sharing and understanding the other person's needs
		➤ Demonstrating genuine concern and caring
⇑	Involvement	Focus of full attention
		➤ Actively listening and observing
		➤ Putting distractions aside when interacting with another person
		➤ Responding to the other person's words, disposition, and concerns
⇑	Awareness	Recognition of individuality
		➤ Recognizing the other person's special characteristics and needs
		➤ Adjusting behavior to the other's presence and personality
⇑ ⇓	Contact	➤ Recognizing the other person's fundamental worth
		Initial linkage
		➤ Showing common courtesy
		➤ Acknowledging the other person's presence
		➤ Establishing a receptive, nonthreatening atmosphere
⇓	Indifference	Passive in reaching out to others or responding to such initiatives
		➤ Withholding of opinion when approached
		➤ Living by the code of the "shrug": who knows, who cares

(Continued)

⇓	Avoidance	Absence of relationship
		➤ Ignoring or not giving another person our attention
		➤ Brushing aside the other person's comments or questions
		➤ Being too preoccupied to notice the other person's presence
⇓	Hostility	Overt or passive aggressive efforts to undermine the confidence in and support of team members for each other
		➤ Withholding of information, cooperation, and support
⇓	Contempt	Intense distraction/anger
		➤ Defiance of individual, team, and organizational goals and performance criteria
		➤ Loss of purpose in relationship
DISCONNECTION		

The *contact* stage provides the turning point from disconnection to connection. Without it, people like Susan Todd and Walter Bingham can be easily swept in a downward spiral from indifference to avoidance, hostility, and contempt. With it, they can begin ascending the ladder from awareness to involvement, empathy, empowerment, and commitment.

Clearly, Bill now wants to move Walter and Susan out of the downward spiral toward disconnection, and he wants Frank and Joan further up the ladder toward connection. Before doing so he would normally apply the Relationship Styles Grid, which we will discuss in the next section, but for purposes of simplification assume that each team member prefers a rather structured and unemotional approach to relationship-building. Bill's scripts for coaching the team toward commitment might run something like those following.

➤ A Script for Coaching an Empowered Person

Bill: Frank, I wanted to talk to you about the project. How are you feeling about the six-month deadline?

Frank: I think we can make it, but we've all got to get on board. We have a lot of potential as a team. In fact, Joan really seems to have a handle on what to do.

Bill: I agree. And I think you and Joan could work as part of a great team. Thanks for the analysis, Frank, and thanks for your enthusiasm. I'm really looking forward to your playing an important role in going forward. *(Reinforce positive behavior and confirm the person's high position on the Connection Ladder. Then suggest a way to move even further towards commitment.)*

➤ A Script for Coaching an Aware Person

Bill: Joan, do you have a minute? I'd like to ask you where you think we stand right now with the project and what our prospects are of meeting our goals.

Joan: I do like this assignment, but I'm worried that we might not have enough time to do it right. And I'm not sure we have the resources we need. But, you know, Frank seems to really have a handle on things.

Bill: I understand your concern, but I'm very glad you like the assignment. I'll bet if you and Frank work together as the core of the team we can make it. *(Confirm the connection by indicating your understanding of the concern, then paraphrase to reinforce your associate's positive observations, building on them to propose a way to strengthen the team and the connection.)*

➤ A Script for Coaching an Indifferent Person

Bill: Susan, do you have a minute? I wanted to ask you about where we stand on the project. What do you think our prospects are for meeting our goals?

Susan: Well, I don't know, I'm just not sure . . . it's not the project so much as Walter and I just don't see how it's possible to pull it off in such a short time.

Bill: I can understand your concern. You've worked with Frank and Joan, haven't you? *(Confirm your understanding and take action. Bill explores ways to connect Susan more fully with the team than with Walter.)*

Susan: Yes.

Bill: Well, they're fairly optimistic. I think we should get you together with them to identify our concerns and prepare an action plan. Let me get back to you shortly on a time, okay? *(Build a connection bridge and offer a specific plan for improvement.)*

Susan: Yes, I guess so.

Bill: Well, I understand your reservation, but we need to work more closely together to take advantage of our team potential to reach this goal. It's certainly important for all of us here. *(Confirm understanding, then lead and connect your associate by offering a positive opportunity and incentive—for Susan, team and individual security.)*

➤ A Script for Coaching a Person Showing Contempt

Bill: Can I trouble you for a moment to ask your opinion regarding the project? Where do you think we stand on the six-month deadline?

Walter: Honestly, I think it's impossible. We're being set up to fail. I don't know how I feel about my work on this project. And I can't see how we can pull it off.

Bill: Well, I appreciate your candor. You know I value your opinion and we both know it's vitally important that we build a cohesive team. Would you think about what problems you see ahead for us, and prepare a list of them for discussion? I think we need to be very concrete about what we say and do. The stakes are high. Okay? *(Reach out a hand of cooperation, but frame the issue and your associate's responsibility clearly.)*

Walter: Yeah, okay.

Bill: I look forward to speaking with you on this later. In fact, I'll get back to you by 2:30 this afternoon. *(Bill establishes a positive basis for either reconnecting Walter or helping him to disconnect and leave with as little negative impact for himself and the team as possible.)*

Though we haven't covered all the levels on the Connection Ladder, these four scripts reveal a few principles that apply to all coaching toward commitment:

➤ Before launching a particular campaign to take action, assess the readiness of the team to move forward.

➤ Praise those highest on the ladder and award them greater responsibility for getting the job done.

➤ Encourage those lower on the ladder to build stronger relationships with those who are more fully committed.

➤ State problems clearly and honestly.

➤ Invite advice about solutions, but always strive for agreement on specific steps that can create greater commitment.

➤ Face threats squarely and develop alternatives to minimize risks to connection.

➤ Tool #2: The Relationship Styles Grid

In actuality Bill would use the Relationship Styles Grid to help him tailor his conversations with each team member. Having determined each person's position on the Connection Ladder, he would formulate communication plans designed to take into account the ways in which each person prefers to relate to others. To reach a person's mind and heart, workleaders know they must deliver a message attuned to that individual's communication frequency.

M-pathic relators can read the needs of people quickly and customize their messages in appropriately different ways. To clarify a person's needs, M-pathic relators determine whether a person tends to operate as a Rational, Intuitive, Functional, or Personal relator.

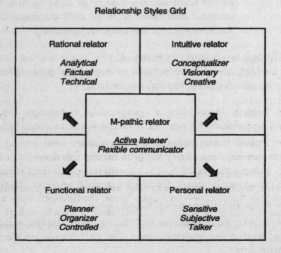

Relationship Styles Grid

Rational relator	Intuitive relator
Analytical *Factual* *Technical*	*Conceptualizer* *Visionary* *Creative*

M-pathic relator
Active listener
Flexible communicator

Functional relator	Personal relator
Planner *Organizer* *Controlled*	*Sensitive* *Subjective* *Talker*

Skillful connectors recognize the legitimate needs of each style of relator. While they also understand their own stylistic tendencies, they try hard to incorporate all the styles into their own repertoire of relationship skills. Over 70 percent of exceptional leaders demonstrate high degrees of competency in three to four styles, which enables them to tailor their messages to others. While people often display blends of these styles, most people do display decided preferences. Understanding these preferences gives workleaders a practical way to implement M-pathic communication.

The Rational Relator

Both structural and rational, *Rational relators* place high value on analysis, facts, and technical expertise. They take great satisfaction in identifying problems, developing a variety of possible solutions, weighing alternatives, and carefully testing options to see what works best. They are typically steady, tenacious functionaries who rely on the scientific method to get things done. Averse to emotionalism and speculation, they often convey skepticism of novel departures from past strategies and practices.

Rational relators frequently delay decisions until they can review the situation carefully and consider all possible alternatives. Other people seek them out for their objectivity and cool thinking under pressure, and they often enjoy a reputation for successfully, if doggedly, getting the job done. They relish their ability to research and plan.

However, they can also seem overly cautious or conservative. Not particularly good at mobilizing others' enthusiasm, they frequently come off as rather cold and calculating. An M-pathic connector will take these tendencies into account when communicating and building a relationship with a Rational relator. The following are some characteristics shared by rational relators:

➤ They think carefully before presenting ideas or opinions. Susan Todd often tells her colleagues, "I'll have to get back to you . . ."

➤ They are goal-oriented and practical. Susan, for example, loves charts.

➤ They successfully separate work from personal life. Susan never takes adversity at the workplace personally.

The Functional Relator

Both structural and emotional, *Functional relators* place high value on planning, organizing, and controlling. They love it when the day hums along like a well-oiled machine, and they exhibit a direct, down-to-earth, energetic approach to work and life when things go according to plan. Highly pragmatic, they enjoy activities that yield concrete, tangible, and immediate feedback. Others often view them as the driving force within the organization because they are consummate *doers* who dig into the details of a project and produce clear-cut results. They commit to an endeavor only after they prove to themselves that the proposed plan will most likely work.

However, their love affair with short-term planning can get in the way of long-range thinking and the evaluation of long-term consequences. Eager to get things done today, they can often lose sight of the way today's actions may create unpleasant repercussions tomorrow. Their behavior can seem impulsive or impatient at times, especially when they try to impose their own agenda to the exclusion of others' concepts, plans, or feelings. The following are some characteristics shared by functional relators:

➤ They feel more at ease in a structured environment. Frank DeLucci works with people more easily when he knows their titles and job descriptions—he is likewise interested in his own.

➤ They are more interested in fine-tuning present organizational practices than in future-oriented concepts. Frank, for example, spent a lot of time redesigning forms, but was not particularly interested in learning how the organization *might* use teleconferencing. "Call me when it's installed," he said.

➤ They feel uncomfortable working on more than one project at once, feeling that they should finish one thing before starting another. Frank will set aside an undertaking to work on a rush project, but he feels this is disorganized.

The Intuitive Relator

Both unstructured and rational, *Intuitive relators* place a high value on concepts, visions, and creativity. Adept at long-range thinking, they tend to gain their greatest satisfaction from entertaining visions of the future. Their imaginations often stimulate those around them. Deep and fast thinkers, they prefer intellectual problem solving over implementing solutions. They challenge those around them with their continuous probing and reexamination, and they earn a lot of respect when their prophecies come true.

Intuitive relators do not feel uncomfortable with disorder and chaos because they are confident that they can grasp the meaning of conflicts, which they view simply as clashes of major forces rather than causes for consternation and worry. Looking at the world from the broadest perspective, they often see relationships between forces that others do not.

However, others can feel frustrated by their freewheeling approach to work and can even interpret all their probing and questioning as acts of hostility. Rather than accepting Intuitive relators as visionaries, others may dismiss them as living in a world of their own. The following are some characteristics shared by intuitive relators:

➤ They prefer to work in circumstances that encourage creativity. Joan Fox prefers brainstorming to structured meetings.

➤ They think in holistic terms and learn processes at a glance rather than step-by-step. Joan has no problem working on several projects at once.

➤ They are often more interested in the evolution of the organization than in fine-tuning present practices. Joan was very interested in the teleconferencing proposal, but had long neglected those forms Frank was working on.

The Personal Relator

Both unstructured and emotional, *Personal relators* place a high value on sensitivity, subjectivity, and interpersonal communication. They relish situations in which they can engage in social-interpersonal contact with others, and they display a deep concern about what others think and do. Skilled at reading between the lines, they listen to what others say and exhibit great patience and forbearance in offering assistance to people experiencing trouble or crisis in their work.

Others see Personal relators as dynamic and stimulating, warm and in touch with their colleagues, and they seek them out to interpret the meanings of behavior or to assess the morale of a group. Others also appreciate Personal relators' ability to anticipate or predict how individuals' feelings may affect a project's outcome.

However, their focus on interaction can also frustrate their co-workers when it seems that Personal relators concern themselves more with the *process* of an interaction than with its *content*. Quite often their reliance on gut feelings causes friction with those who prefer a more objective approach to a situation. The following are some characteristics shared by personal relators:

➤ They strive to maintain a friendly demeanor. John Neal, a new hire, believes that being pleasant is an indispensable element of professional behavior.

➤ They much prefer working with a team to working alone. In fact, John becomes bored and restless working by himself, but he's a highly motivational team leader.

➤ They exhibit strong concern for others' feelings. When John replaced Walter Bingham in the department, he was very careful about stepping into Walter's duties and commitments.

Returning to the team we introduced earlier, Bill Johnson has moved Frank DeLucci, Joan Fox, and Susan Todd toward higher levels of commitment and has replaced Walter Bingham with John Neal, who brings a lot of enthusiasm to the team. Bill has determined that Susan is a Rational relator, Frank is a Functional relator, Joan is an Intuitive relator, and John is a Personal relator. At this point Bill needs someone to accomplish a short-term goal, the creation of a new report for a critical meeting on Friday. He knows Susan will want to take plenty of time researching optimum formats; Frank will want to get it on Bill's desk before the end of the day, Joan will want to express her creativity, and John will not feel comfortable doing the report on his own. In Bill's scripts for dealing with each person's needs, note the use of such *connecting phrases* as "I understand," "That's interesting," or "I know we can do this" to reinforce connection by confirming that what has been said was heard or that what has been said is a positive step up the Connection Ladder. We'll explore connection phrases more thoroughly in the next section.

➤ A Script for Dealing with a Rational Relator

Bill: You know that new report we've been discussing? I'd like to see a draft at our meeting on Friday. *(State a clear objective.)*

Susan: I don't know if that will give me enough time to consider the possible formats and find the best one.

Bill: I understand the time limitations. Well, let's see. Today is Monday, so you can research past reports today, with the goal of isolating the most effective formats we've used in the past. Then you can spend Tuesday and Wednesday designing the new report, which will give you Thursday to fine-tune it. Okay? *(Empathize and allow sufficient time for the task.)*

Susan: Yes, that should give me plenty of time.

Bill: I'll write down everything the report must accomplish and have it on your desk within the hour. *(Writing the assignment down will help the Rational relator accept concrete objectives.)*

➤ A Script for Dealing with a Functional Relator

Bill: You know that new report we've been discussing? Could you put together a preliminary design by this afternoon? *(Provide an interim goal that allows for a quick sense of accomplishment.)*

Frank: I'm sure I can.

Bill: I knew you could. Then we can study it to see if anything needs revision. Can you get any revisions done by Wednesday? *(Confirm the connection and the goal. Then build in time for correction.)*

Frank: That's plenty of time.

Bill: Great. Then Susan and Joan can give it a look-over. By Friday you can have a perfect report for the meeting. *(Allow time for others to provide input.)*

➤ A Script for Dealing with an Intuitive Relator

Bill: You know that new report we've been dis-cussing? How would you like to take the idea and run with it? *(Stress the opportunity for a cre-ative, visionary approach.)*

Joan: Sounds great. I'd love to come up with some-thing radically different this time.

Bill: That's terrific. Just please bear in mind that everyone must buy into it on Friday. To sell any-thing radically different you might research past reports as benchmarks. What do you think? *(Reinforce connection. Allow for a creative ap-proach, but ground the work in practicality.)*

Joan: I already have an idea for a new format I think people will like.

Bill: I knew you would. I'll stop by your office around three o'clock each day until Friday, just to see how the project is progressing. *(Praise and follow up regularly to keep the project reasonably grounded.)*

➤ A Script for Dealing with a Personal Relator

Bill: You know that new report we've been dis-cussing? I'd like you to take charge of it, but I thought you might like to get Joan and Frank involved. *(Permit work with others, but suggest someone whose objectivity might balance the team.)*

John: That would be great. Joan and I work really well together, and Frank always dots the "i"s and crosses the "t"s. We'd make a good team.

Bill: Friday will roll around sooner than we'd like. Perhaps I could sit in on your first meeting this afternoon. And I'll stop by your office Wednesday to see how you all are doing. *(Emphasize realistic, concrete goal for the project; offer personal help and interaction.)*

John: That's a good idea. See you at three. I'd better go and see Joan and Frank right now.

➤ The M-pathic Relator

M-pathic relators, having mastered all four basic relationship styles themselves, recognize those styles in others and use that recognition to say just the right thing at just the right time. Rather than simply coping with different styles of communication, they learn to actually communicate in each style. Like serious students of a foreign culture, they don't merely visit the tourist attractions, they learn the language so they can actually immerse themselves in the culture. M-pathic relators learn the relationship languages of others and immerse themselves in the daily reality of their work lives. As a result, whenever M-pathic relators engage others, they speak clearly to their intellectual and emotional needs—not just to make them feel good, but to move them up the Connection Ladder to total commitment. By doing so, they relate successfully to a wide range of people, assemble balanced teams, and gain the respect of everyone they contact.

Though real-life situations will contain many more subtleties and nuances, the preceding scripts and the following case study highlight a number of important principles to keep in mind as you develop your M-pathic communication skills:

➤ Assume that every word and gesture counts.

➤ Design all communications to raise levels of commitment.

➤ Take the initiative to make contact.

➤ Tune in by designing your first statement to meet individual needs.

➤ Ask questions and invite both positive and negative feedback.

➤ Keep all messages as simple and straightforward as possible.

➤ Communicate clearly and consistently with all stakeholders.

➤ Praise and reward connection; address disconnection quickly and decisively.

Marliese Thatcher, one of the most interesting workleaders who emerged from our research, exemplifies the role of the connector. Her story vividly demonstrates M-pathic communication's power to turn around even the most fractured and demoralized organization.

➤ Making the Right Connections— Marliese's Story

Among all the leaders we have met over the years, Marliese Woerner Thatcher stands out because of her success in connecting with people who have been torn apart by anger and turmoil. Marliese came aboard one of the Southwest's premier healthcare providers, University Hospital in San Antonio, to restabilize a complex academic medical center faced with financial chaos and fractious and embittered stakeholders. How she met the challenges of political posturing by city, state, and federal officials; a disenfranchised medical staff; insecure workers and desperate union leaders; a shell-shocked board of directors; and fearful patients is a remarkable story.

The saga began shortly after World War II when Marliese, at the urging of her family, accepted a foreign student scholarship and left a still devastated Hamburg, West Germany, to study chemistry and nursing at Johns Hopkins University. During her junior year she met and married a newly appointed assistant professor of microbiology, left school, and settled into the relatively leisurely and uneventful life of a faculty wife. Six years and four children later, however, a tragic plane crash left her widowed and without resources. Unwilling to burden her family in Germany, she went to work as a nurse's aide while finishing her undergraduate studies and subsequently pursuing two graduate degrees in microbiology and business.

Like her fellow workleaders, Marliese reached out to connect to the world in a way that would permit her to serve both her family and others. During the course of the next thirty years she raised four children, gained the respect and gratitude of colleagues at every level of work life, and eventually rose to the presidency of one of the world's largest healthcare management companies.

During her tenure as president of that firm, Marliese was approached by University Hospital's Board chair for help; rather than pass the mess off to someone else, she accepted the project of stabilizing the situation. At once she began to pursue a classic connection strategy.

First, she assessed the challenge. To identify precisely where communication had broken down she met personally with physicians and employees and administered a global Mission Effectiveness Assessment survey to more than 5,000 patients; 4,000 employee associates; 1,500 physicians; 2,000 community, governmental, and accrediting agency representatives; the Board; union leaders; and vendors. To each group she posed a series of detailed questions designed to get at the heart of two overriding issues: Is University Hospital fulfilling its mission of service? If not, why not? The answers helped her not only to identify global problems but also to understand the needs of each of the stakeholder groups.

A key finding of research into the connector role is that stakeholder groups can assume collective identities, including characteristics of connection/disconnection and relationship styles. This occurs when individuals who share a specific agenda for action perceive that they must bind together more closely to achieve it. This phenomenon occurs every day in the world of politics, where people subordinate their individual differences to take on a collective identity that advances their self-interest. It is the force behind unions and professional associations, class action suits against corporations, the home town loyalty of football fans, and the conviction of religious and ethnic groups.

In everyday work life, the stresses and strains of individual lives can play out in group lives too. When they do, the group takes on characteristics that represent the nature of its members' concerns and uses their talents and resources in the best way to advocate for them. Marliese's story is an interesting case in point. As a result of her extensive research, including the objective survey assessments, fact finding, and focus group meetings, Marliese was able to scientifically show her colleagues that different stakeholder groups had clearly assumed collective identities. While individuals in each group might have different relationship styles in their personal lives, these were being subordinated to the needs of the group.

Physicians were acting as Rational and Functional relators, banding together to find a rational model for reestablishing control in an organization where they had traditionally been able to exert strong functional control. Employee associates were acting as Personal relators, turning to each other and the union out of frustration at being rebuffed by everyone else. Managers were performing as Functional relators, trying to find security by fulfilling tangible objectives that affected everyday work life. The Board was behaving as an Intuitive relator, projecting a visionary ideal of what the hospital could and should be as solace for what it apparently was. And patients were acting as Personal and Functional relators, turning to each other to fight the system for the care that many of them would otherwise not receive.

This was both good news and bad news for Marliese. The fact that stakeholder characteristics and needs could be

defined with reasonable confidence as group qualities gave
her the capacity to develop efficient connection strategies
for building bridges of communication. The fact that stakeholders were banding together to that extent, however, indicated that they were frustrated with the hospital's failure to
meet their individual needs. The irony of the situation was
not lost on Marliese, who observed that, "We exist to meet
individual needs, but neither the individuals we served nor
the individuals providing service acted individually. The
fear at University was so great that individuals had sought
the protection of their group. I had to reach out to them as
groups before I could connect with them as individuals. If I
had lunch or dinner with a physician or Board member, the
moment we moved away from personal discussion to discussing the hospital, they put on the mantle of their group."

For 45 intense days, Marliese surveyed and listened to
advice, opinions, and stories while accumulating mountains
of data. Then, using the results, she positioned each of University Hospital's key stakeholders on the Connection Ladder:

The Connection Ladder

	Connection	Key stakeholder position:
	Connection	
⇑	Commitment	
⇑	Empowerment	
⇑	Empathy	
⇑	Involvement	Board and vendors
⇑	Awareness	Patients
	Contact	
⇓	Indifference	
⇓	Avoidance	Med staff and associates
⇓	Hostility	Union
⇓	Contempt	
	Disconnection	

Using the Relationship Styles Grid, she recorded each stakeholder's style and formulated an initial connection strategy:

Stakeholder	Present Situation	Relationship Style and Connection Strategy
Patients	Quality and commitment are perceived to have declined. Evidence of fear and increasing unwillingness to return to the hospital for care.	*Personal and Functional relators:* Reassurance needs to be provided through intensive customer education and empowerment, including clinical, technical, and legal information.
Med staff	Demand rational explanation for crises, but want to retain personal control regardless of the explanation, without investing significant commitment.	*Rational and Functional relators:* Deliver a rational wake-up call that reveals the risk of losing functional control. Provide path to reinvest to reestablish position.
Associates	Grieving for co-workers lost in downsizing combined with fear over loss of jobs and control. Influence of unions could precipitate drop to hostility and contempt levels.	*Personal relators:* Reframe the challenge in terms of possibilities—that the glass is half-full. Reconnect associates through involvement in team problem solving and work redesign.
Managers	Feel overwhelmed and adrift. Downsizings increased workload and disrupted established structure and procedures.	*Functional relators:* Reaffirm and clarify their role to reestablish sense of structure and include them in setting priorities and planning their own future.
Union leaders	Fear loss of control on work and personal levels. Overtly aggressive and moving toward contempt—defiance and slander.	*Personal and Functional relators:* Call the challenge by presenting rational analyses of the financial and clinical challenge coupled with reaffirmation of patient care commitment. Challenge them to join constructively in the process.
Board	High levels of commitment based largely on esteem associated with role in the past. Most lack rational understanding.	*Intuitive relators:* Provide multidimensional reality orientation to reshape expectations and redefine Board responsibilities.
Vendors	Reasonably supportive but evidencing anxiety over the hospital's ability to pay. Recognize traditionally strong role of hospital as customer.	*Functional relators:* Reawaken personal bonds of loyalty through historical review of payment and sharing of plans for restabilizing. Emphasize potential as a viable customer.

Though Marliese worried about the connection levels of all stakeholders, she knew that her efforts must start with the hospital's customers—its patients. Not only were patients increasingly unwilling to return, but—most alarmingly—morbidity and mortality rates (incidences of illness and death in the hospital) had been climbing. Both the survey and focus groups convened to examine the situation revealed that although patients believed they were receiving adequate care, they doubted the hospital's ability to sustain it.

To address the challenge, Marliese employed M-pathic communication designed to mobilize people to action quickly and efficiently. She began by assigning the task of redesigning the hospital's interaction with patients to newly formed cross-functional patient education work teams. In addition, she invited the president of the medical staff, dean of the faculty, and board chair to join her on local TV and radio programs, to conduct interviews with newspaper reporters, and to participate in internal patient videos designed to communicate a message of commitment and renewal. Marliese scheduled these efforts concurrently with town hall style forums for physicians and employees, discussions she guided with highly focused M-pathic scripts. She coopted leaders of key constituencies by inviting them to join her in reviewing the data and in designing appropriate and meaningful messages to build bridges of understanding. Watch how Marliese approached some of her stakeholders.

➤ A Script for Connecting with Dr. Smith, a Rational Relator

A strong believer in collaborative decision-making, Marliese invited the president of the medical staff to help her design a town hall meeting with physicians. During her meeting with Dr. Smith, who she knew would project the Rational relator needs of his physician group, she followed a script attuned to his style and his level of connection. A portion of that meeting's transcript went as follows:

Marliese: Doctor, from our research, and from my conversations with physicians, I sense they want a clear explanation of our financial situation and the risks it could represent to their investment of energy and commitment. Would you agree? *(Marliese introduces her diagnosis as both a message and a question targeted to a Rational relator. She frames her message in terms of research and individual physician feedback. Her question uses a rational phrase—"clear explanation"—to probe underlying emotional sensitivities. She establishes a beachhead to build connection.)*

Dr. Smith: Well, yes and no. We've heard so much already, I'm not sure anybody wants to hear any more. *(He attempts to disconnect and assert control by putting Marliese on the defensive.)*

Marliese: That's interesting. Could you help me understand what you're saying? What information do you think physicians need? *(Marliese uses a bridging statement to reconnect. Then she redirects the responsibility by asking him to work through his apparent indifference and avoidance.)*

Dr. Smith: Well, here's the story. We're tired of all the politics and funny-money games that executives and the board play. I don't think physicians will get involved unless they can really get inside what's going on and reclaim some measure of control. *(He responds and makes contact, venting his anger and disclosing his real fear: loss of control. In this way, he also*

> *reveals his real needs and the criteria which must be met for the relationship to move further up the Connection Ladder. This provides Marliese with the information she needs to build an effective bridge for communication.)*

Marliese: I think I understand. Are you suggesting that physicians do want financial facts and that they want to get involved in the budget and policy-setting process, perhaps with someone like you as their formal representative participating in decision making? *(She sets the commitment hook. She moves the relationship up the ladder to empathy, reaffirming—with "I understand"—and reinforcing the connection by repeating his concerns in the form of a question, which requires him to commit, even tentatively.)*

Dr. Smith: *(She reels him in.)* That's a good idea, I think. . . .

Marliese used her assessment of the relationship to develop an opening dialogue targeted to Dr. Smith's Rational relationship needs. She did this by asking a question that placed responsibility on him to commit more fully. Like a skilled tennis player, she set up the situation so she could eventually drive home a decisive and winning point.

➤ A Script for Connecting Front-Line Employees, Personal Relators

In the following short exchange excerpted from a transcript of a meeting with employees, Marliese designed her opening comments to meet a different and more complicated challenge. Employees had banded together out of frustration at not having their needs met by the organization they had come to rely on as a home. They were also turning to the union to fulfill intense personal needs. Unstructured feelings of personal loss combined with deep fear over the potential loss of their own jobs to create an explosive situation. Many employees had lost friends through panic-driven and sloppily implemented downsizings. Recognizing the need to establish a connection beachhead with so many Personal relators, Marliese chose to begin the meeting by empathizing with their dilemma.

Marliese: Thank you for taking the time from your heavy workload to join me. As many of you have already told me, decisions of the past make today's situation that much more challenging. Your presence here is proof of your deep commitment to making this organization successful. Meeting here today starts that process, one that I would like to ask you to help shape by advising me on how to conduct the town hall meetings for employees. Do you think we should begin with a thorough review of our financial situation or with a discussion of the very important quality improvement and work redesign challenges we need to meet? *(Marliese makes contact, beginning the movement towards commitment by stating her awareness of past problems and the importance of associates' previous and future contributions. She then sets the stage for involvement by asking questions that move people toward a sense of service and away from self-interest. While she indicates empathy and a willingness to empower through shared decision making, she tries to help associates move beyond their anger by focusing on opportunities for positive action and commitment. She realizes she must get an achievement agenda on the table even if it doesn't elicit full commitment at*

> *first. By framing it as a question, she both invites*
> *participation and puts the responsibility for posi-*
> *tive behavior on their shoulders. She also indicates*
> *that she recognizes the real need to get past the*
> *destructive behaviors of the past.)*

Associate: Ms. Thatcher, we think the most important thing is that you tell us the truth. We feel like mushrooms, we're kept in the dark and fed manure. *(The associate resists Marliese's outreach with a mildly oppositional response that cleverly avoids responsibility and throws it back on Marliese's shoulders.)*

Marliese: I can understand how you feel. I keep a pair of boots in my office myself for whenever I need to wade through board and administrative staff meetings. Precisely what kind of information do you need? I certainly want to provide you with the knowledge you need to meet these challenges. *(She uses a bridging phrase to maintain the connection, followed by an empathetic and humorous parody that deflects the implied personal attack, which could have provoked a hostile response. This enables her to maintain her connection and transform the potential attack into an opportunity for information sharing—empowerment—and reinforcement of the responsibility of service that is the basis for their commitment.)*

➤ A Connecting Script for Nurse Managers, Functional Relators

Nurse managers sent Marliese a formal invitation to attend their biweekly meeting to discuss a range of issues including budget deadlines, union harassment, and control of work assignments. As a former nurse herself, Marliese understood that the managers were turning to the everyday functional requirements of the job to establish some form of control. She understood their Functional relationship needs and mind-set: how to get the job done. She began her remarks by recognizing the structural and emotional need of the Functional relator to control a situation.

Marliese: Thank you for your invitation to be here and for your carefully organized list of issues. Before beginning, however, I'd like to ask the chair of the meeting how you would like to proceed. *(She makes contact by honoring their need for control while informing them of her own preparation and similar concern.)*

Chair: Ms. Thatcher, our most pressing concern is how to get more done with less, in less time with less support. We'd appreciate hearing how you expect us to get all of this done. *(The chair reveals the hostility that Functional relators can feel when their orderly, controlled world is disrupted. She reveals the intense emotional concern that Functional relators often bring to their interactions. Marliese now has a diagnosis and chooses to defuse, empathize, and propose a new structure to confront the sense of growing chaos.)*

Marliese: I understand your feelings. I have walked in your shoes and I must say that I agree with your implied conclusion: I don't think any of us can do more with less, in less time with less support. Your comment opens up an interesting opportunity. We must instead do things differently, very differently. If I might, I would like to ask for your assistance in helping me refine a plan for setting clearer priorities and redesigning work systems, including staffing practices. I've prepared a draft plan for your reaction and development, if you think that would be appropriate. (*Marliese bridges—"I can understand"—and turns their opposition into an opportunity for moving up the ladder to involvement. She does this by ignoring the hostility in the chair's comment while picking up on the insightful assessment contained in it. In this way, she rechannels energy from moving down the ladder toward contempt to moving upwards toward commitment. She reinforces this through a strong act of empowerment that feeds their need for structure—a plan—and for control—in "your development." She then concludes with a commitment to building a strong relationship by offering them the opportunity to decide.*)

➤ A Connecting Script for the Board, Intuitive Relators

The board of University Hospital is composed of prominent business and civic leaders who joined it to feel pride and accomplishment for being part of a visionary effort. They had just completed a strategic vision for the hospital that outlined a broad array of new and high tech services to be housed in a new $500 million campus. But they were frustrated by what they considered to be petty operational details that were derailing implementation of the vision that they intuitively believed was the only viable future for the hospital. Marliese had been charged with addressing this vision. Recognizing a classic Intuitive relator profile, she realized that she must help them move from the abstract to the present reality.

Board member Samantha Pelletier:	Marliese, how soon do you think we can get on track and start to implement our strategic vision for University? I

think we need to remember the visionary mission we've set out to accomplish,
capturing the power of twenty-first-
century science to address the human
needs of our community. When will we
begin to see progress? *(Samantha reveals
the Intuitive relator's visionary needs by
posing an apparently simple question that
can only be answered by addressing complex issues. Avoidance of the question will
be interpreted as an act of hostility, but
attempting to answer it as stated could
lead to a complex and potentially adversarial debate. To connect, Marliese needs
to both honor the intuitor's insight and
connect her to others whose views she may
not have considered, thus appealing to her
interest in acquiring more information.)*

Marliese: Samantha, thank you for putting the
most important and complex question
for this board back on the table. Harnessing the full potential of this organization can and should, as you point out,
lead to progress. I understand your concern, as do many others here at University who also want to get back on the
road to progress. I don't have a precise
and complete answer for your question.
But I do have the beginnings of one. It is
embodied in my report on what I have
found out about the strengths and weaknesses of our organization from the
people who work here and from those
who receive our services. I think it provides an accurate assessment of the sta-
tus of our vision. I'd like to share it with

you and the board as a starting point for getting back on the road to progress. (*Marliese makes contact by praising Samantha's commitment then uses a bridging statement to connect Samantha and other board members to other stakeholders. At the same time, rather than confront Samantha regarding the relevance of her assessment of priorities, she uses the assessments of others to do so. Here she also uses strategic humility to acknowledge that she does not have a "precise and complete answer," but she does have "the beginnings," thus reducing the risk of disconnection that could arise from avoiding Samantha's question.*)

Marliese's interactions illustrate how a workleader can efficiently and effectively assess a situation and respond rapidly with scripts that connect the right people to the right cause at the right time. In recognition of this skill and her wonderful sense of humor, her colleagues gave her a Norman Schwarzkopf Rapid Response Award at her recent retirement dinner.

■ FULFILLING THE ROLE OF THE CONNECTOR

When we compare Marliese Thatcher's approach to connection with that of other workleaders in our study, we find some clear patterns. First, workleaders spend time assessing commitment levels and relationship styles with the express goal of pinpointing and closing gaps between present and desired levels. With this goal in mind, they meticulously craft their communications, choosing language their target audience can understand. This may sound obvious, but most people find it hard to scale up their vocabulary for one audience and scale it down for another. An audience of physicians may well require an in-depth technical explanation, while an audience of patients may require a less complex nontechnical presentation. Workleaders listen carefully to the language of others and try to use phrases that touch their minds and hearts.

To improve connection, think in terms of *strategy and tactics*. Given a *strategy* to build maximum commitment, select *tactics* that move people up the Connection Ladder. Once workleaders make contact and begin to move people off the downward spiral that leads to contempt and disconnection, they work diligently to escalate people through the stages of awareness, involvement, empathy, empowerment, and, finally, commitment. Clear questions that prompt clear answers accomplish more than strong statements, orders, or pleas for cooperation.

The workleaders in our study were all skillful Multipath relators. Once they defined their stakeholders (their different audiences) and assessed the connection positions and needs of each, they modified their message to move everyone up the Connection Ladder. In the case of University Hospital, within 18 short months Marliese Thatcher's connection program moved the organization from the brink of bankruptcy and clinical shame back to its historical role as a premier center for care and teaching, with a burgeoning bottom line to sustain progress.

Selection puts the right people in the right place at the right time, and connection links the right people to the right cause. However, when it comes to getting the work done problems always arise. The next role, that of the problem solver, explores how workleaders resolve problems swiftly and permanently to produce results.

4

The Problem Solver

During a landmark operation at Johns Hopkins in 1945 an astonished anesthesiologist watched as a dying six-year-old boy, born a "blue baby" with a sickly blue complexion, suddenly turned a healthy pink, his lips a cherry red. A distinguished surgeon, Dr. Alfred Blalock, had performed an experimental operation on the boy that would revolutionize medicine and save tens of thousands of lives. He had gotten the idea from a colleague, Dr. Helen Taussig. Dr. Taussig was not a surgeon herself, but a pediatric cardiologist whose own heart had been broken countless times as she performed the sad duty of examining cyanotic or "blue" babies after they had died.

Cyanosis was an almost always fatal condition for newborns. As early as the 1930s Dr. Taussig realized that many blue babies were born with a heart defect that prevented blood from reaching the lungs to pick up sufficient oxygen for the body. When she saw Dr. Robert Gross perform an operation at Children's Hospital in Boston to *reduce* blood flow to a cyanotic baby's lungs, a solution to the problem dawned on her: Why not build a blood vessel to *increase* circulation? Dr. Gross thought this idea feasible, but his conventional medical training prevented him from trying it.

In the 1940s Dr. Taussig finally found a willing surgeon in Dr. Blalock at Johns Hopkins. The experimental surgery worked beautifully, and when news of the accomplishment reached the press requests began to flood in from desperate parents around the country. During the next six years, Dr. Taussig saw more than 3,000 children in her clinic, and Dr. Blalock and his associates performed more than 1,000 life-saving operations.

Many thousands of children owed their lives to Dr. Taussig's operation before the heart-lung machine made open-heart surgery at first possible, then almost routine. Her vision opened up the whole field of cardiac surgery and emboldened surgeons to develop techniques never dreamed of before. The technique she invented became known as the Blalock-Taussig operation, and it earned Dr. Blalock election to the National Academy of Science in 1946—an honor not bestowed on Dr. Taussig until 1973.

Ironically, Helen Taussig suffered from discrimination throughout her early career. Although Harvard's School of Public Health admitted women in the early 1920s, it did not allow them to take degrees. Harvard Medical School did not admit women at all, and only allowed them to take special courses with an instructor's permission. Helen took a histology course, for example, but was forbidden to speak to the male students.

However, she continued to work tirelessly on solving medical problems. In the 1950s she worked with Dr. Frances Kelsey at the U.S. Food and Drug Administration to keep thalidomide off the U.S. market, and thus spared parents in this country the heartbreak suffered by European parents when thousands of severely deformed thalidomide babies were born in the 1950s and 1960s.

In 1959 she became a full professor at Johns Hopkins, in 1964 she was the first woman elected President of the American Heart Association, and in 1972 she was the first woman to become Master of the American College of Physicians. In addition to election as a Chevalier of the French Legion of Honor and receiving the U.S. Medal of Freedom, she accepted 20 honorary degrees and was inducted into the Women's Hall of Fame in Science in Seneca Falls, New York. Though officially retired from Johns Hopkins in the 1970s, she continued to work an eight-hour day until shortly before her death.

■ THE ROLE OF THE PROBLEM SOLVER

Like other accomplished leaders uncovered in our study, Dr. Helen Taussig was unwilling to define any problem as unsolvable.

Our research uncovered the fact that excellent leaders spend most of their time—60 percent—solving problems. They spend another 30 percent fulfilling the other seven leadership roles, which often merge with their problem-solving efforts. Only 10 percent of their time involves maintenance activities such as routine paperwork. In short, they focus on their overriding mission and invest the bulk of their time and energy fulfilling that mission.

This contrasts with average leaders who spend less than 30 percent of their time problem solving and over 45 percent of their time on maintenance activities involving paper and procedural work. They become so trapped in the complexity and bureaucracy of their organizational systems that they can not break free to focus on their most important responsibilities—namely, solving problems for customers and colleagues. Breaking free from the trap of routine and bureaucracy requires initiative. High Leadership IQ people aspire to take control of their lives and avoid letting others control them. They provide a role model of individual responsibility in the workplace.

The best problem solvers use a simple analytical process to keep their work responsibly focused. Like a Beethoven melody, the progression of this analytical process becomes so logical and powerful that it plays successfully in many different settings with many different players. The following chart provides an outline of how this process works:

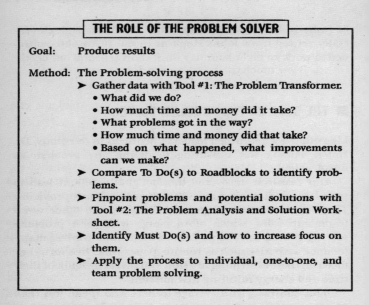

THE ROLE OF THE PROBLEM SOLVER

Goal: Produce results

Method: The Problem-solving process
➤ Gather data with Tool #1: The Problem Transformer.
  • What did we do?
  • How much time and money did it take?
  • What problems got in the way?
  • How much time and money did that take?
  • Based on what happened, what improvements can we make?
➤ Compare To Do(s) to Roadblocks to identify problems.
➤ Pinpoint problems and potential solutions with Tool #2: The Problem Analysis and Solution Worksheet.
➤ Identify Must Do(s) and how to increase focus on them.
➤ Apply the process to individual, one-to-one, and team problem solving.

Problem solvers are scientists. They search for data that will help them identify opportunities for change, and look behind the bureaucratic facade of procedure and protocol for real problems and workable solutions. As one of the leaders in our study said, "When it comes to the tough challenges, I always try to follow the admonition 'In God we trust, all others must use data.' " To help produce data and keep themselves focused on real problems, problem solvers rely on two simple tools, the *Problem Transformer* and the *Problem Analysis and Solution Worksheet*.

➤ Tool #1: The Problem Transformer

Both Dr. Taussig and contemporary problem solvers ask five questions that help them transform problems into opportunities.

The Problem Transformer

1. What did we do?
2. How much time and money did it take?
3. What problems (roadblocks) got in the way?
4. How much time and money did the problems consume?
5. Based on what happened, what should we do?

Dr. Taussig learned from her experience examining victims of cyanosis that in order to achieve better results, she needed to go beyond conventional wisdom—to study why traditional approaches had failed and look for new pathways to achievement. She utilized a disciplined process of analysis and, knowing she couldn't do it alone, she enlisted the help of Dr. Blalock and his associates. With Dr. Taussig's guidance they built a strong team relationship based on openness and commitment, always holding themselves accountable for achieving their goal by documenting their efforts and noting all successes and failures. Then they evaluated the results and identified solutions that moved everyone further toward the goal—even if it meant doing away with earlier advancements, such as Dr. Gross's techniques.

Contemporary leaders follow the same path. Let's examine how the Problem Transformer provides a script for problem-solving leadership in the front lines of work.

➤ A Problem-Solving Script for the Front Lines: Part I

Ricardo, or "Ric," the newly appointed manager of one store in a twelve-store retail bicycle franchise, has grown concerned about a problem on the sales floor: Two couples, a student, and a family group are all browsing, but there is only one salesperson, Lisa, to assist them all. And she's in the stockroom assembling a point-of-purchase display. Ric approaches Lisa.

Ric: Lisa, what's up?

Lisa: I'm putting together another display.

Ric: Can you take care of that later? We've got a floor full of customers now. *(Ric quickly identifies and solves an immediate problem—lack of customer service—but knows that he must address the circumstances that caused it.)*

Lisa: Sure thing.

Ric: Ask me about this display later, when you get a chance. I'm curious about it. *(Ric arranges for a later discussion of the problem.)*

In this brief vignette, we've seen Ric ask the first question of the front-line problem-solving script: "What are you doing?" Then he interrupts the script in order to focus Lisa's attention on the customers, making sure, however, that he delegates responsibility to Lisa for resuming their discussion later.

By midafternoon, during a lull in business, Lisa comes looking for Ric.

Lisa: Ric, you wanted to talk to me about that display.

Ric: Yes. Thanks for getting back to me. Do you have twenty to thirty minutes before things heat up again? *(Ric establishes connection with Lisa and clarifies her availability for a problem-solving meeting.)*

Lisa: Yeah, sure, this is the lull before the storm hits again—about an hour from now.

Ric: Okay. Here's what I'd like to do. I'd like to ask you to help me with a little problem solving, using the display as a starting point. Okay? *(Ric empowers Lisa and enlists her assistance as a fellow problem solver, thereby strengthening the team.)*

Lisa: Sure. How does it work?

Ric: We need to ask five basic questions. What are you doing? How much time does it take? What are the things that get in the way—your roadblocks? And how much time do they take? We'll record the information on a sheet of paper and then, separately, we'll ask: Based on what we know, what can we do to improve things? Let's start with the display. How long does it take you to put it together? *(Ric takes a blank sheet of paper and creates a Problem Transformer.)*

Lisa: About an hour and a half, maybe two.

Ric: Is this becoming a standard part of the job or a roadblock that's just come up?

Lisa: Oh, no. We've been doing these for six months or so, as long as I've been here. Jill said that our vendors used to set up displays, but most have stopped doing that.

Ric: Well, let's put it down as a To Do for the moment. How often do you put displays together? *(Ric begins to guide Lisa's problem solving.)*

RIC'S PROBLEM TRANSFORMER DATA COLLECTION WORKSHEET

What did we do? (To Do)	Set up displays
Time it takes	1½–2 hr. each
Roadblocks (problems that get in the way)	Interruptions
Time consumed by roadblocks	Add 30–45 minutes to each display setup

Lisa: Oh, I'd say a couple a week, because the other stores have been asking me to do it for them as well.

Ric: Well, that's interesting! So that makes three displays a week totaling four and a half to six hours. Is that about accurate? *(Ric affirms Lisa's involvement and also her responsibility for the validity of the data and for participating in the problem-solving practice by asking her to confirm the information she gave.)*

Lisa: Yes, but I'm a little shocked by the time. Maybe it's a little off. I'm working part-time now and that's a third of the time I spend here!

Ric: Don't worry about strict accuracy for now, we're getting a general picture that's very helpful. That's enough information to move to the next step and ask ourselves what we should do differently. Can you offer any general observations on what we've discovered before we move on to the really important question of what to do differently? *(Ric continues to increase Lisa's involvement in the process by delegating observation responsibilities to her.)*

Lisa: Well, I'm supposed to be getting paid for sales but that's *not* what I'm really doing—I'm a go-for, doing everything else or messing around with roadblocks. It's crazy. No wonder my commissions are way down.

Ric: That's a breakthrough Lisa! You can see how the way we organize our work can help us or hurt us. Do you think we've learned enough to try and figure out what to do about it? *(Ric reinforces Lisa's observation and their mutual stake in finding solutions and sets the stage for a transition to the fifth question.)*

Lisa: Absolutely. I know we can fix this problem.

Ric: Terrific. Let's start to develop some answers to the question: Based on what we now know, what improvements can we make? Let's analyze our problem more closely.

➤ Tool #2: The Problem Analysis and Solution Worksheet

During a relatively brief 20-minute dialogue, we have seen Ric and Lisa move from discovery and definition of a problem to a point where solutions can begin to emerge. Answer-

THE PROBLEM ANALYSIS AND SOLUTION WORKSHEET	
Must Do activities (goals)	**Time it takes**
1._____	_____
2._____	_____
3._____	_____
4._____	_____
5._____	_____
Activities that get in the way (roadblocks)	**Time it takes**
1._____	_____
2._____	_____
3._____	_____
4._____	_____
5._____	_____
Should Do activities (solutions)	**Time it takes**
1._____	_____
2._____	_____
3._____	_____
4._____	_____
5._____	_____

ing the question, "Based on what we now know, what improvements can we make?" is a critical stage in the problem-solving process, one that Helen Taussig and other workleaders enter armed with knowledge and determination.

Drawing data from the first four questions in the Problem Transformer, the problem solver sorts activities into three categories:

1. Must Do activities (goals)
2. Activities that get in the way (roadblocks)
3. Should Do activities (solutions)

➤ A Problem-Solving Script for the Front Lines: Part II

Ric moves Lisa to the next stage of problem solving by focusing their attention on what the data from the Problem Transformer mean for achieving the one goal essential to their mutual success: customer sales and service.

Ric: Lisa, the question is, based on what we now know, what can we do to improve things? To address that big question, let's ask: What must we do, and how do we increase the time spent doing that? Let's zero in right now on our main goal and try to come up with ways to achieve it. What's your number one Must Do priority? *(Ric draws Lisa's attention to her number one responsibility, thus clarifying her primary responsibilities.)*

Lisa: That's very clear to me now: customer sales and anything related to it.

Ric: Okay. Let's put customer sales down as the number one Must Do. How can *you* increase the time you spend on it?

Lisa: Well, frankly, by dropping whatever else could interfere and serving the customer first. That makes customer service my main To Do and makes setting up displays a big roadblock.

Ric: Bingo! I think you have a very clear sense of your priorities. There's only one reason we're really here. Anything that gets in the way of customer service has got to be moved out of the way, streamlined, or eliminated. Right? *(Ric applauds Lisa's insight, reinforcing its value, her role, and his expectations of her. He then takes her to the next stage, which includes a thorough analysis of the problem and a sharing of the responsibility for solutions.)*

Lisa: Absolutely.

Ric: Good. Well, let's follow through and identify our roadblocks and what we should do to overcome them. Let's make sure we assign clear responsibility for improvement. We're all in this together. After we're done, I'll meet with the rest of the team individually as well. Okay, let's put our analysis together. *(Ric explains how the problem-solving process is central to overall team effectiveness, orienting Lisa toward her individual responsibility for service as well as to her connection to the whole team. They complete the Problem Analysis and Solution Worksheet and produce a practical plan for action.)*

Ric: Well, Lisa, I think we've made a good start on addressing this problem. It looks to me like we've got a problem-solving plan we can put into action right now. And everyone should benefit. If we spend seventy-five to eighty percent of our work week with our customers, the quality of our service and our productivity should rise a solid eighteen percent.

RIC AND LISA'S PROBLEM ANALYSIS AND SOLUTION WORKSHEET

Must Do activities (goals)	**Target time**
1. Customer sales	14 hours of an 18-hr work week

Activities that get in the way (roadblocks)	**Time it takes**
1. Setting up displays	6 hours a week

Should Do activities (solutions)	**Time it takes**
1. All Salespeople: Ask vendors to set displays up	½ hr.
2. Ric: Hire temporary help to set up displays if necessary	20 minutes (+ wage)
3. Ric arrange: Rotate displays that have been set up in other stores in the chain	1½ hr for the set up of one display

Lisa: One thing's for sure, I've got a better handle on what my priorities need to be to do it.

Ric: Me too. Perhaps we should go through this exercise more regularly. How about we meet next week for fifteen to twenty minutes to review our solution to this problem and tackle another one? Can you think of any other time wasters that get in your way?

Lisa: Yeah. That new PC network. It's full of bugs.

Ric: Okay. Let's put that on our agenda. Hey, we've got some customers coming in. Let's get going! *(Ric has moved Lisa through the process to a point where she can take action to solve a problem. He also clarifies his expectations for follow-up and suggests that problem solving become a more conscious, continuing part of their work.)*

➤ Problem-Solving for the Patient—Dori's Story

Dori Martingloria is nurse manager of an oncology (cancer) unit at one of America's leading medical centers. She has been committed to serving others for as long as anyone can remember. While she won't speak for herself on this issue, others do and the story they tell is one of unfailing dedication and pragmatic problem solving that inspires everyone around her to respond to even the most difficult challenges. From her early education as an RN to her Ph.D., Dori has retained a love for work at the patient's bedside. Now, facing the challenge of restructuring the oncology unit she spent seven years building into a world-class team, she knows she must draw on her deepest reservoir of resolve.

Dori has just received the compiled results of a special Problem Transformer Assessment in which she asked her staff to list their To Do(s) for a one-week period of time. As she reviewed them she began to complete a Problem Analysis and Solution Worksheet. Under Must Do activities (goals) she wrote, "Deliver even better service despite recent operational downsizing." She intends to discuss the results with her leadership team in a Work Redesign meeting devoted to identifying and solving serious service and financial problems.

During the meeting Dori will use a central question to focus everyone's attention on solutions: "Are the right people in the right place at the right time and cost to deliver quality patient care?" The workers most affected by this question are the registered nurses (RNs), whose hourly wage is 50 percent higher than practical nurses' and 100 percent higher than nurse assistants' (NAs) and secretaries' wages. How can the team reduce labor costs by at least ten percent *without* reducing quality of care? Dori starts the meeting with Jim, Melissa, and Paul by focusing everyone on that goal.

Dori: Good morning. Well, as we all know, the subject today is how to restructure and redesign our unit so the right person is in the—

Jim, Melissa, and Paul: *(In unison.)* Right place at the right time and cost for quality.

Melissa: Dori, you've got us quoting that phrase in our sleep.

Dori: Thank God. We'll need to remember it given our challenge today. I've assembled all the input from our special Problem Transformer Assessment. Everyone told us what they're doing and a whole lot more. We'll use it to help us make important redesign decisions to meet the goal we've been discussing for the past few weeks: namely, to reduce labor costs by ten percent more and still maintain high-quality care.

But before handing the data out, I'd like to ask each of you to help me with a special exercise. It involves two parts. First, I'd like us to describe the profile of a typical patient on our unit and what his or her concerns might be. Then second, I want us to look at the work through that patient's eyes. Jim, you've been working with patient satisfaction and profile data. Describe a patient for us. *(Dori demonstrates deep commitment to the mission and her team by framing what she knows will be a difficult problem in the context of their shared responsibility to the customer—the patient.)*

Jim: Okay. I've been reading a lot of our patients' comments, so I think I can give you a patient's point of view. Let's say I'm a fifty-four-year-old man just admitted to this unit with prostate cancer. I'm pretty nervous about what type of treatment I'm going to receive, but I don't want to panic. My concerns are: Can anyone tell me what's going on and what my options are? How are the surgical and chemotherapy procedures carried out? What are the chances that treatment will be successful? I'm probably also worried because my assessment interview was done by a female resident physician half my age and I've had to put up with interminable delays for every aspect of my treatment so far, which causes me a lot of stress.

Paul: Jim, I feel stressed just hearing you put those perceptions together. Is that what our patients are feeling?

Dori: Yes, I've read their evaluations and so should everyone. Jim paints a realistic picture. Let's take his case study and ask ourselves this: If we were that male patient and making decisions here, what work would take highest priority? How do we achieve our goal—our Must Do—of delivering the highest-quality care despite recent and future downsizings? I'll keep track of the comments on the Problem Analysis and Solution Worksheet. *(Dori focuses the team on the core issue, involving them and building shared responsibility through this exercise.)*

Paul: Well, I'd put patient assessment, education, and counseling at the top of the list.

Melissa: I agree, but I'd add giving medication, especially chemotherapy.

Paul: You'd better note physician support, too. And if we're thinking of this from a patient's point of view, we have to add such nitty-gritty things as room cleanliness, staff courtesy, and promptness.

Dori: Excellent! Anything else? *(Dori leads the team through an intensive ten-minute Problem Analysis session.)* Now, before going any further, let's take a look at the Problem Transformer data we compiled that shows us what everybody is *actually* doing. Let me call your attention to one fact. Our RNs reported that they are spending less than twenty-five percent of their time on the Should Do(s) you just identified. I just circled them to draw your attention. The data also showed that RNs spent a considerable amount of time on such activities as general clerical duties, feeding, getting supplies, housekeeping, toiletting, linen change, transportation, and bathing, as well as on more appropriate activities such as patient assessment, medication, patient counseling and education, and physician support. All in all, their jobs were complex—they reported forty-four activities—and stressful. With this data and our Must Do(s) in mind, what are your observations? What are the roadblocks, the things that get in the way? *(Dori hands out the results of the special Problem Transformer report that compares the percent of time nurses spend on the top 15 time-consuming activities in their job with the percent of time others spend doing the same work.)*

Melissa: Well, I know I should say "Oh my God," but I'm really not surprised. We have a virtual role reversal of responsibilities. The nurses spend too much time on clerical and other activities that shouldn't be a part of their job, like getting supplies. And I'm afraid that this situation exists all over the place, not just here on oncology.

PROBLEM TRANSFORMER REPORTS FOR DORI'S ONCOLOGY UNIT

Percent of Time Spent on Top 15 Work Activities by RNs Compared to Others

Activities	RNs	Practical Nurses	Nurse Assistants	Secretaries
General Clerical	8%	6%	3%	33%
Patient Documentation	7%	9%	7%	—
Patient Assessment	6%	12%	14%	3%
Feeding	5%	3%	4%	7%
Getting Supplies	5%	7%	3%	6%
Clinical Procedure	4%	10%	—	1%
Housekeeping	4%	4%	6%	7%
Toiletting	4%	2%	4%	2%
Linen Change	3%	2%	5%	2%
Medication	3%	6%	3%	—
Patient Counseling	3%	4%	7%	4%
Transportation	3%	4%	6%	4%
Bathing	3%	7%	4%	—
Physician Support	3%	6%	6%	3%
Patient Education	2%	5%	6%	9%

Paul: Exactly right. We have our most expensive people, our RNs, doing the support work.

Jim: But remember, I'm the patient. I still want someone to talk to me about my condition and to make sure my linen's clean. I say we need to get our nurses refocused by redistributing and eliminating unnecessary work, but making sure there's qualified staff available to provide good care.

Dori: Wait a minute, let me get this down on the Problem Analysis Worksheet. Okay. I agree and I'd like to ask you one more set of questions. *(Having moved the team to a stage of high involvement and empowerment, Dori decides to move further.)*

Paul: Oh no. I don't know if I can take it!

Dori: Relax, Paul. These are very direct and logical. I'd like to propose that we consider the almost unthinkable—namely, reducing the number of our RN staff to accomplish two things: first, to free some dollars to get more support staff. This way we can make sure that the patient's linen is always clean, that meals are served while they're still hot, and that someone always answers a call bell. We can hire several NAs if we cut only a few RN positions. Second, this support staff will allow us to focus more of an RN's time on the Must Do patient care work that only they are qualified to do. As you'll notice, between the percentage of time RNs are spending on support work and other things, well over forty percent of their time and our labor dollars is wasted. They're not doing nurses' work but other work. Making it possible for nurses to do the work they're supposed to be doing benefits everybody, especially the patients. *(Dori pushes forward to the next and most difficult level of the problem—cost reduction.)*

Paul: Hold on, Dori, now we're treading on sacred territory. How do you justify that move?

Dori: With the data. And this data came from our staff who have told us that RNs' jobs are so fragmented that they're not focused on core responsibilities, which means that the *quality is threatened*. And this is just as relevant: The quality of life for RNs is suffering because of

	high stress due to the lack of focus on patient care and the fact that their job is so complex by comparison with others.
Melissa:	It's true. The data does justify those conclusions.
Jim:	And I think the staff already understands the situation as well. After all, they're the ones who gave us this data.
Dori:	That's what I've been thinking. In order to address patients' concerns as Jim outlined them for us, and the work design problems our data has revealed, we have to take some definite steps like the Should Do(s) we've ended up with on our Problem Analysis and Solution Worksheet. Take a look: Does it sum things up and point us to a solution? *(Dori brings the team back to their original goal of finding solutions for delivering quality care.)*
Jim:	It's tough, but accurate. Unless we get our nurses refocused, patient care will suffer.
Melissa:	And the cost issue really makes things clear. We're paying top dollar for our nurses to do the wrong work.
Paul:	Yeah. But there are going to be some really skeptical people out there who are not going to like these results.
Dori:	I agree with all of you. We do have to get our nurses focused and use our money more responsibly. And yes, Paul, there is skepticism which I would like to suggest we meet head-on. We'll have to conduct problem-solving sessions like this one for our physicians and staff in order to involve them in the process. Paul, which sessions do you think should come first?

DORI'S PROBLEM ANALYSIS AND SOLUTION WORKSHEET FOR JIM'S CASE STUDY

Must Do activities (goals)

1. Deliver even better service despite operational downsizing

Activities that get in the way (roadblocks)

1. Reversal of responsibilities for the RN

2. RN role doing clerical work and getting supplies

3. Nurses not focused on their real job

Should Do activities (solutions)

1. Refocus nurses on:
   - Patient assessment
   - Patient education
   - Patient counseling
   - Giving medications (chemotherapy)
   - Physician support

2. Redistribute support work from nurses to others, and . . .

3. Consider reducing the number of RNs to hire more support staff

---

(Dori has used the problem-solving process to research the issue and suggest a solution she has been mulling over. But she knows there are several practical issues that need to be addressed before implementation, including the issue of resistance, which Paul represents. She pulls Paul in by turning his natural skepticism to good use. To do this, she uses the technique of asking Paul to react to some options rather than giving him an open-ended question that might cause him further anxiety and stimulate an oppositional response.)

Paul: Either or both, as soon as we've got our act together. This is too important to wait any longer. In fact, I'd use this same exercise you used with us. When they look at this through the eyes of the patient, it makes things much more clear.

Dori: Thanks, I agree. Let's figure out how we can go about it.

Dori spends another ten minutes with the team planning the next steps. She knows it's vitally important to conclude every problem-solving session by establishing a practical course of action. Like Ric and Lisa, she used the Problem Transformer to gather data, she used this data to define the problem, and then she and her team developed potential solutions through the Problem Analysis and Solution Worksheet.

■ FULFILLING THE ROLE OF THE PROBLEM SOLVER

In accord with Saint James's observation, "Faith without works is dead," Dr. Taussig, Ric, Lisa, and Dori and her team defined a group's worth in terms of its capacity to translate its members' commitment—their faith—into action by solving problems in the front lines of service. To address these problems, workleaders employ a simple adaptation of the scientific method to discover and define problems and to create solutions that transform the way they work. The two tools presented in this chapter, the Problem Transformer and the Problem Analysis and Solution Worksheet, keep attention focused on discovering, defining, and solving problems.

From Dr. Taussig's historic breakthrough in the treatment of cyanotic children, to Lisa and Ric's redesign of contemporary work priorities, to Dori's insights into the restructuring of patient care in the 1990s, workleaders tackle the most challenging problems head-on. They involve their fellow workers in directly addressing the most vital issues in their work lives. In the process they consider such pivotal issues as delegation, work stress, customer focus, and work responsibility. To maintain their own focus, workleaders spend over 60 percent of their time on problem solving, often combining problem solving with other roles to ensure integration of their efforts and to guarantee results. Above all, workleaders use the problem-solving role to strengthen their commitment and optimism and to prepare their co-workers for the opportunity to attain a synergistic kick of achievement. Such achievement sets the stage to expand and strengthen the organization through the role of the evaluator, the subject of our next chapter.

5

The Evaluator

On August 15, 1947, India broke free from 200 years of British colonial rule and became an independent nation. Though many of the country's 250 million people had longed for that day, one man more than any other made it possible: Mohandas Gandhi.

Members of the Gandhi family had long been employed as Indian prime ministers, working with their British rulers as administrators of local governmental affairs. As the youthful Gandhi observed his father and the other members of the family at work, he saw that advancement depended greatly on pleasing the English, an observation that drove him to convince his family to let him study law in London. When Gandhi arrived in London in 1888 he was so impressed and awed that he began to adopt English habits, "playing the English gentleman"—as he put it later—by dressing nattily in top hats, silk shirts, and spats, and carrying a silver-topped cane.

After receiving his law degree in 1893, he took an opportunity to work on a complicated commercial case in South Africa. His assignment was to last only one year, but as it turned out Gandhi stayed on in South Africa for twenty-one years to fight for civil rights. Two memorable incidents that occurred soon after he arrived changed his life forever.

The first happened during his first day in court as he began to familiarize himself with the workings of the local justice system. Several minutes after entering the room he realized that the Magistrate was glaring at him. His turban, it turned out, offended the judge, who ordered him to remove it immediately. Equally offended, Gandhi refused and left the court. His client later explained to him that his refusal to remove the turban was an act of civil disobedience: He had actually broken a law against non-Western forms of dress. Incensed over such discriminatory practices, Gandhi wrote a letter of protest to the newspapers.

The second incident took place on a train trip to Pretoria, for which Gandhi had purchased a first-class ticket. At the Maritzburg station along the way, a white passenger entered the cabin, took one look at the young Indian with whom he was to share it, and left—only to return with two railway officials. The officials ejected Gandhi on the pretext that while he had paid for a first-class ticket for the entire overnight trip, he hadn't paid for overnight *accommodations*.

One degradation followed another, and before long the humiliation caused by systematic prejudice changed the young lawyer's whole perspective on ambition. Rather than go along with a perverse system, he dedicated his life to changing it. English laws, he concluded, protected only the English, and while South Africa's perversion of democratic principles was more blatant, the laws governing India were no less stifling and divisive.

Instead of advancing his own career as advocate and servant of the system, he would use his knowledge of that system to advocate the rights of his people. Setting aside his self-interest, he began to pursue justice for all. Only one week after the Maritzburg train incident, Gandhi called a rally of Indians in South Africa to campaign against racial and ethnic discrimination. His first public speech at that rally laid the foundation for far-reaching efforts to follow. Thousands joined his cause and, like Gandhi, learned to fight for civil rights peacefully. Determined to fight on the battlefields of law and reason, he simply refused to obey discriminatory laws, always pleading guilty to charges of civil disobedience. Consequently, he spent a lot of time in jail, both in South Africa and later in India. The injustice of his incarceration only served to hold the system up to ridicule and increase his influence. In an Indian jail in 1932 he fasted to push the government into action against the unfair treatment of Untouchables, and within one week the government acceded to his demands.

Gandhi's great tool in the fight against oppression was holding the behavior of nations up to fair evaluation, to reveal that the system and those who had designed it—the English in particular—should be held accountable to the universal principles of justice they claimed to uphold. Before evaluating others, however, Gandhi evaluated himself. Before he presumed to urge others to change their lives, he changed his own.

Gandhi's humility and unwavering commitment earned him the love and respect of a nation, and his tactics won him respect around the world as a brilliant social strategist. His accomplishments hinged, more than anything else, on his fulfillment of the role of the evaluator.

■ THE ROLE OF THE EVALUATOR

Evaluation is an act of strategic humility. It requires both competence and the knowledge that improvement can and should be achieved. Like Gandhi, high achieving leaders view evaluation as a positive act, an opportunity to identify ways to harness the potential of all people more fully. Gandhi was a competent leader secure in the knowledge that improvement would only come about if he humbly accepted the responsibility of making it happen. One of the most significant revelations of our leadership research is that successful leaders structure their efforts around evaluation, and develop strategies that flow from careful, ongoing measurement of situations. The following comments show how strategies for success flow from evaluation.

➤ *A sales manager for a computer firm:* "I used to have a real problem with evaluation. You know, 'Judge not lest you be judged.' I felt it was arrogant to judge others. Then I realized that judging them wasn't the issue—customer service was. When I evaluated someone I was not evaluating them as a person but as an instrument of service to something bigger than both of us. I'm not evaluating them for me but for the customer who pays both our salaries."

➤ *A nursing team leader:* "I can't nurse my nurses in addition to my patients. Only they can improve themselves. My job is to make sure they understand and take part in assuming that responsibility."

➤ *A Fortune 100 CEO:* "Everyone can grow if you give them the right information. My job is to see that my team understands what works, what doesn't, and why."

Together, these observations support the five principles of effective evaluation.

The first element is *purpose:* evaluation for whom? In a democratic and capitalistic culture, the customer has the final word on whether a product or service will be purchased or a politician returned to office. So it is only sensible to perform evaluation with the customer in mind.

The second principle is *responsibility:* Who owns responsibility? Each worker owns responsibility for personal conduct because only that person can improve his or her individual behavior. This leads to the third principle: *involvement.* Who should get involved in evaluation? Every worker. People excluded from the evaluation process will never feel responsible for any improvement strategies that flow from the evaluation.

The fourth principle is *guidance:* Who channels important efforts? Workleaders shoulder the responsibility to guide and teach others, helping individuals understand the need for greater achievement. Ownership depends as much on understanding as it does on involvement.

The fifth principle is *service:* Whom does the workleader serve? The customer and those who serve the customer. The effective evaluator bestows praise and recognition for superior service and provides counseling with regard to poor service. Such counseling should aim to improve service, but if it fails to accomplish higher levels of service it can result in removal of an individual's responsibilities.

The evaluation process moves outward from the individual to the team, the organization, and in the case of Gandhi and other statespersons, to the nation and the world community. Evaluation for its own sake is inadequate. All evaluation must be transformed into individual acts of improvement. This particular insight helps explain many of the problems corporations, government agencies, and nations experience with their assessments. Unless an assessment leads to higher standards of performance, it will fail. Too often those in high bureaucratic positions blame the system, the policy, or the procedure for performance failure when they should be concentrating on people. People, not systems and procedures, take action.

And people, not systems, are accountable for results. Our research showed that the best leaders refuse to hide behind the cover of the organization and insist, instead, on careful evaluation of their own personal behavior and the behavior of each individual with whom they interact. This unequivocal belief in the power of personal accountability contrasts starkly with the faceless bureaucratic evaluation practices that have undermined public confidence in so many business, charitable, and governmental institutions.

People with high Leadership IQ share an optimistic belief in the potential of individuals to improve, grow, and adapt. To them, evaluation is a means to an end. Average leaders, by contrast, see evaluation as a bureaucratic chore filled with accountability traps that can ensnare the unwary.

Our comparison of the evaluations conducted by workleaders to the evaluations practiced by average leaders revealed clear differences. Most notably, average leaders fail to recognize outstanding performance and tend to force all associates into a narrow scoring range, a practice that reflects an unwillingness to go on record in support of outstanding performance. Average leaders also experience three times the rates of turnover and absenteeism as workleaders, and exit interviews revealed that this turnover runs especially high among employees who are outstanding achievers.

By contrast, the most successful leaders create a magnet of positivism that attracts top performers and motivates others to achieve higher levels of service. Their evaluations utilize two tools: the *Key Principles for Effective Evaluation* and the *Performance Appraisal Worksheet*. They apply these tools to all levels of the organization, moving out from the individual to teams and the organization as a whole. Before we explore these tools, consider the following composite view of the role of the evaluator:

THE ROLE OF THE EVALUATOR

Goal: Enhance individual performance

Method: Diagnose levels of service and use performance appraisals to create improvement strategies

➤ Center evaluation on the customer.
➤ Emphasize individual responsibility and accountability.
➤ Involve all workers in their own evaluation.
➤ Establish a context with Tool #1: The Key Principles of Effective Evaluation.
➤ Conduct a preparatory meeting before applying the evaluation.
➤ Design improvement strategies with Tool #2: The Performance Appraisal Worksheet.
➤ Guide the process through the Appraisal Script.
➤ Develop a concrete schedule for evaluation.
➤ Use the same process with workers, teams, customers, and the organization as a whole.
➤ Create a magnet of positivism by identifying and recognizing performance that serves the mission.

➤ Tool #1: The Key Principles of Effective Evaluation

The first step is to establish a context for evaluation by defining its purpose—what we are going to evaluate and why we should do it. Alicia Harris, cochair of an innovative corporate evaluation design team for a rapidly growing environmental services company, explains why so much depends on clearly establishing the purpose: "Each of us in this company, from the secretary to the CEO, knows that what we do—handling hazardous wastes—can affect the lives of many people. That's *why* evaluation is so important. It focuses us on our purpose for being in business, on what is vital to our success. This has led us to define *what* needs to be evaluated to achieve that purpose. All of our stakeholders, from the board to stockholders, employees, and—most importantly—customers, participated in defining our corporate purpose and breaking it out into four categories of performance evaluation. They include evaluation of individual service to customers and to the team, stewardship, and technical role competency. The discussions that led to these four categories and the principles that guide the process were so informative that we built discussion of the evaluation process as preparation for individual evaluations." These four categories of performance—though sometimes referred to by different names—were also considered the core categories by 97 percent of our workleaders. We therefore expanded on these core performance categories and combined them with the five principles of evaluation to develop Tool #1 for effective evaluation. We generalized Alicia's approach to create an education tool any workleader can use. An effective evaluation addresses all stakeholders' involvement in the following key areas (see chart).

To see an evaluation guided by these principles in action, picture Valerie Johnson, a lab manager at Envirolabs, as she discusses performance evaluation with Al Bronkowski, a member of her department. The discussion precedes an evaluation meeting that will take place in a few days. Wanting to

---

THE KEY PRINCIPLES OF EFFECTIVE EVALUATION

1. Define the purpose, the *what* and *why* of evaluation.
   - ➤ Why—to serve customers
   - ➤ What—to perform outstandingly in four areas:
     - Service to customers
     - Service to the team
     - Stewardship
     - Technical expertise
2. Increase responsibility for outstanding performance.
   - ➤ As individuals
   - ➤ As a team
   - ➤ As an organization
3. Involve each individual worker.
4. Guide and teach to develop potential.
5. Serve those who serve through positive reinforcement.

---

get Al deeply involved in the process, Valerie uses the five principles to prepare Al for a positive experience.

➤ A Script for Involving the Individual in Evaluation

Val has chosen an informal and collaborative setting for the meeting with Al. Moving from behind her desk, she sits alongside Al at a work table so that she can share the information she wants Al to review. She addresses Al courteously in a low-level, relaxed voice.

Val: Al, thank you for arranging your work so that you could join me to discuss the evaluation process. As I mentioned at our staff meeting, all of us in the company participate annually—and more often at times. The first thing we do is discuss what we're going to evaluate and why. After this discussion, we'll get into the mechanics of the evaluation itself. Okay? Do you have any questions? *(Val immediately applies Principle #1: Define the Purpose, which establishes a framework for the meeting and minimizes the anxiety that any evaluation process can cause.)*

Al: Just one. Are we going to do the evaluation right now?

Val: No. We'll do the evaluation in a week or so, after we've decided exactly what we're evaluating and why. *(She reinforces the need to understand what's going to happen and why.)*

Al: Okay. So what is it we're evaluating? *(Al reacts skeptically.)*

Val: Service and the specific behavior it takes to deliver it. In consultation with customers, employees, and the board, the company has committed itself to examining distinct categories of performance in the evaluation process. These are: first, individual service to customers; second, service to team members; third, stewardship, including attendance and efficient use of staff and resources; and last, technical competency in specific work roles. *(Val defines the purpose of the company in concrete behavioral terms that translate an abstract concept of purpose into practical behaviors for which each worker has responsibility, thus also applying Principle #2: Increase Responsibility.)*

Al: Well, doesn't evaluation really just come down to whether you know how to play the game? *(Al seems slightly hostile and sarcastic.)*

Val: Good question. You tell me, Al. Let's consider a different setting than our own, say a hospital. Would you want to be in the hands of a brilliant doctor who doesn't show up? Or a nurse who told you to bite the bullet when you asked for pain medication? Or a lab tech who forgot to share information with your physician regarding blood tests? *(Val reinforces the need for evaluation—Why?—and then points Al's mild hostility in a more positive direction by asking him a question that reinforces his responsibility and need to become personally involved—Principle #3. She thus turns the negative energy embodied in his hostile response into a positive force, teaching Al Principle #4, how to understand the importance of evaluation in our lives.)*

Al: I can see what you mean about a hospital, Val, but I'm not likely to kill anyone from my stool in this lab. *(Al is trying to disconnect and avoid responsibility.)*

Val: I see your point, but you may be underestimating your importance to the team and our customers. Al, do others depend on you for accurate results? *(Val uses a bridging phrase to maintain a connection with Al. She continues with a compliment that also reinforces his responsibility, which she then further reinforces by inviting him to describe his own individual responsibilities and to see that these constitute service to the customer and the team.)*

Al: Sure, but it's not life or death. *(A more intense and direct disconnection effort.)*

Val: Could the results of your tests reveal a health problem for the public? If you didn't accurately perform the tests, could our clients sue the company for failure to fulfill our responsibilities? If the results were wrong or late, would our co-workers be put in a huge jam when preparing reports? How would you answer these questions, Al? *(Val* *now meets the challenge head-on. By establishing connection based on civility and understanding, she can assert the power of her commitment to leverage Al toward becoming more fully involved. Her questions touch on how Al's work performance and technical competency affect expenditure of staff time and resources.)*

Al: Sure, all of those bad things *can* happen. Okay, I get it. We're connected to each other by performance responsibilities, whether we like it or not.

Val: Precisely, Al. You're important because what you do or don't do can have real effects on other people's lives. That's why I'd like to ask you to take this Performance Appraisal Worksheet along. I'd like you to read it carefully and try your hand at evaluating your own performance. If you have any questions regarding items under each area, see me or bring them along when we get together next week. I'll be completing the same worksheet on your performance and we'll compare results, okay?

Al: Okay. I'll probably stop by and ask questions beforehand.

Val: Terrific. I'll be available whenever you need me. I'm looking forward to meeting with you next week. *(Val moves to closure through positive reinforcement— Principle #5—of Al's responsibility—Principle #2—to become involved—Principle #3—in fulfilling the purpose of the organization—Principle #1. Throughout, she transforms avoidant and hostile behavior into positive energy for growth and development by guiding and teaching—Principle #4—which she continues to reinforce by her ongoing commitment—"I'll be available whenever you need me.")*

➤ Tool #2: The Performance Appraisal Worksheet

The preparatory discussion of the Key Principles of Effective Evaluation sets the stage for conducting a performance appraisal interview. The Performance Appraisal Worksheet is used during the interview to guide the evaluation process. The following chart distills what we learned about the way workleaders fulfill the evaluator role. Their performance appraisal scripts tend to follow the worksheet fairly closely.

Notice how the Performance Appraisal Worksheet includes all four of the crucial service categories defined in the purpose: service to customers, service to team members, stewardship for human and material resources, and technical work role competency. These four categories of performance emerged as universal categories for evaluation in the eyes of our workleaders. Now let's see how the process works by listening in on Jim Jochum's meeting with Joanne Bailey, a member of his housekeeping team at a five-star resort hotel.

➤ A Script for Conducting A Performance Appraisal

The week before the appraisal interview, Jim walked Joanne through the various steps of the Performance Appraisal Worksheet, and told her he would complete one himself. A week later Joanne, whose performance had been slipping, joined Jim in his office. For the following exchange they sat side by side at a small work table.

Jim: Joanne, thank you for making time in your busy schedule to meet with me. I've been looking forward to this chance to review things together. I know it's very difficult to think about work performance in the midst of the

Performance Appraisal Worksheet

Directions: Indicate the extent to which the associate demonstrates the following service skills.

Scoring
1 = Low   10 = High

	Associate	Workleader	Final

I. Individual Customer Service Skills

	Associate	Workleader	Final
• Responsibility—provides ethical service, does not allow personal or organizational issues to interfere with fulfillment of customer needs	☐	☐	☐
• Timeliness—provides responsive service	☐	☐	☐
• Sensitivity—provides emotional support and understanding	☐	☐	☐
• Accuracy—demonstrates clear comprehension of needs	☐	☐	☐
• Coordination—provides service in the right sequence	☐	☐	☐
• Thoroughness—meets the full range of customer needs	☐	☐	☐
AVERAGE SCORE:	☐	☐	☐

II. Team Service Skills

	Associate	Workleader	Final
• Respect and courtesy (Contact)	☐	☐	☐
• Awareness of others' needs (Awareness)	☐	☐	☐
• Willingness to become involved (Involvement)	☐	☐	☐
• Empathy and understanding of others' needs (Empathy)	☐	☐	☐
• Willingness to share information (Empowerment)	☐	☐	☐
• Follow-through on work responsibilities (Commitment)	☐	☐	☐
AVERAGE SCORE:	☐	☐	☐

III. Stewardship Skills

	Associate	Workleader	Final
• Is present and punctual	☐	☐	☐
• Utilizes financial and material resources efficiently	☐	☐	☐
AVERAGE SCORE:	☐	☐	☐

IV. Technical Service Skills

	Associate	Workleader	Final
Skill #1:	☐	☐	☐
Skill #2:	☐	☐	☐
Skill #3:	☐	☐	☐
Skill #4:	☐	☐	☐
Skill #5:	☐	☐	☐
AVERAGE SCORE:	☐	☐	☐

(Total scores for each section and divide by 4) TOTAL SCORE: [＿＿＿|＿＿＿|＿＿＿]

V. Comments

VI. Improvement Contract

VII. Signatures ＿＿＿＿＿＿＿＿＿＿＿   ＿＿＿＿＿＿＿＿＿＿＿

Performance Appraisal Worksheet for Joanne and Jim

Directions: Indicate the extent to which the associate demonstrates the following service skills.

Scoring
1 = Low   10 = High

	Joanne	Jim	Final

I. Individual Customer Service Skills

	Joanne	Jim	Final
• Responsibility—provides ethical service, does not allow personal or organizational issues to interfere with fulfillment of customer needs	8	6	☐
• Timeliness—provides responsive service	5	5	☐
• Sensitivity—provides emotional support and understanding	8	8	☐
• Accuracy—demonstrates clear comprehension of needs	6	6	☐
• Coordination—provides service in the right sequence	7	4	☐
• Thoroughness—meets the full range of customer needs	9	6	☐
AVERAGE SCORE:	7	6	☐

II. Team Service Skills

	Joanne	Jim	Final
• Respect and courtesy (Contact)	6	8	☐
• Awareness of others' needs (Awareness)	7	7	☐
• Willingness to become involved (Involvement)	8	8	☐
• Empathy and understanding of others' needs (Empathy)	8	7	☐
• Willingness to share information (Empowerment)	8	5	☐
• Follow-through on work responsibilities (Commitment)	5	5	☐
AVERAGE SCORE:	7	7	☐

III. Stewardship Skills

	Joanne	Jim	Final
• Is present and punctual	6	7	☐
• Utilizes financial and material resources efficiently	6	6	☐
AVERAGE SCORE:	6	6.5	☐

IV. Technical Service Skills

	Joanne	Jim	Final
Skill #1: Environmental skills	7	8	☐
Skill #2: Work schedule management	7	8	☐
Skill #3: Security skills	7	8	☐
Skill #4: _____	☐	☐	☐
Skill #5: _____	☐	☐	☐
AVERAGE SCORE:	7	8	☐

	Joanne	Jim	
(Total scores for each section and divide by 4) TOTAL SCORE:	7	7	

V. Comments

VI. Improvement Contract

VII. Signatures _____   _____

work day. Did you have any difficulty filling out the worksheet? *(Jim establishes a communication beachhead with Joanne through courtesy and empathy for her work situation. In the process, he establishes a tone of responsibility and focuses their attention on the task at hand. He gently but pointedly engages her in the appraisal process by emphasizing the worksheet.)*

Joanne: I wasn't sure about all the questions, but I tried.

Jim: Good. We'll address the difficult areas as we go along. Let's begin by reviewing the worksheet together. We'll review each section and examine those areas where we see things similarly and then move to the others. Okay? *(Jim offers positive reinforcement at the first stage of the review, keying into areas of agreement which, even in the case of low scores, affirms Joanne's willingness to accept responsibility for her work.)*

Joanne: Thanks. It's a lot easier to deal with some of these items.

Jim: I know, for both of us. The interesting thing is that each of us has strengths and weaknesses, but our most important strength is the willingness to try and improve, which you've already shown. *(Jim turns a simple response into an opportunity to guide and teach, an act that empowers and affirms their connection.)* Well, let's see. If we compile our scores on one worksheet, we can get started. *(Jim uses a simple clerical task to focus Joanne's attention on the worksheet, which now becomes an agent in the discussion and helps reduce tension and anxiety. Jim literally points to the paper as he proceeds, engaging Joanne personally with direct eye contact. Together, they note the emerging pattern of agree-*

ment and disagreement, strengths and weaknesses.) Joanne, let's pick some of these items for discussion, starting with some areas of agreement. For example, I agree with you that you demonstrate outstanding sensitivity to customers. Tell me a little about how you do it, would you? *(Jim consciously selects high scores as a starting point, striving to lead through positive reinforcement. He doesn't lock in one performance category, but moves around to encourage Joanne's self-examination.)* As we look at these scores, it really appears that we have a similar view on many things, like our agreement that your timeliness, accuracy, and follow-through leave something to be desired. Let's talk about each one briefly, okay? What about the timeliness issue?

Joanne: Well, I've had some trouble getting any work done on time because I keep getting dragged away to do something else.

Jim: I didn't realize that was a problem. Please tell me more. *(Whenever possible, Jim asks Joanne her opinion first. Often, as in this case, he learns about a problem he didn't realize existed. As Joanne finishes, Jim asks her to address another item.)* Joanne, what about accuracy?

Joanne: Well, sometimes I'm just not careful enough.

Jim: I agree. I've noticed that you don't always dot the "i"s and cross the "t"s. What do you think you can do about this? *(Jim continues to use positive reinforcement while encouraging Joanne to assume responsibility for improvement.)*

Let's move on to a touchier item where we seem to have a difference of opinion. For example, I've observed better performance than you have in coordinating things. I've seen significant improvement here recently. At the same time, I think thoroughness has suffered. Maybe you're relying on others to do too much. What do you think? *(Jim moves into a more sensitive area by combining it with a positive assessment. He offers a possible explanation, which gives Joanne an opportunity to think things through without challenging Jim personally. Jim proceeds through the review, moving from areas of agreement to disagreement, from strengths to weaknesses. He concludes the session by comparing overall scores.)* Joanne, overall, it looks like we have a pretty similar view, and we've identified some areas for improvement. Some of these belong to all of us as a team. For example, I appreciate the information you shared on the timeliness issue. Others, like accuracy and thoroughness, belong in your hands. Would you agree?

Joanne: Well, yes, I would. I can see I've got some work to do there.

Jim: Well, I'd like to suggest we think about a couple of these areas overnight and then wrap up the appraisal in a brief meeting tomorrow. I'll bring my final scores but I can tell you they're not going to be very much different than what we've got. I'm going to change my score on timeliness but stick pretty much to the others. Would you agree that's reasonable? *(Jim could either move to closure right now or give Joanne and himself a little time to think things over. The more controversial the discussion, or the more reflective the worker, the more sense the latter approach makes. He asks Joanne to acknowledge his observation, even if she doesn't agree, and*

> *then gains her commitment to a concluding meeting.)*

Joanne: Yes, that's reasonable.

Jim: Good. I'd also like to ask you to think about any comments you would like to add to the worksheet and some ideas for improvement— perhaps some changes in accuracy and thoroughness. I'll be proposing that we focus on strengthening those areas as part of an individual improvement contract.

By using the Performance Appraisal Worksheet as a tool for action, Jim maintained a positive, constructive connection with Joanne even as they began to address some rather serious problems in her performance.

Eleanor Lamberth, a prominent labor attorney and one of our exemplary leaders, commented on how such an appraisal form can create and preserve a productive work environment. "More grievances are made and lost because of imprecise evaluation than anything else. When a leader has to write a lot, rather than address a logical and carefully prepared form that ties right into the core mission of the organization, it suggests that little thought and preparation has gone into it and that little common practice exists. Inconsistencies result and the leader is the one who ends up being evaluated, driving a wedge of anger and blame between workers on all levels."

In addition to providing a concrete form for recording observations, the Performance Appraisal Worksheet also supports the use of a carefully constructed script, which Jim implemented quite skillfully. His interview proceeded logically through three phases.

➤ *Phase I: Consolidate worksheets.* Jim started by consolidating scores on one worksheet. Some workleaders use this tactic as a collaborative warm-up, establishing an atmosphere of practical problem solving that sets the right objective tone at the outset. It also nonverbally focuses attention on the worksheet itself, highlighting the rational and professional responsibilities involved in the evaluation process rather than the potentially subjective and emotional issue of authority. It establishes an adult/adult forum (Let's talk), rather than a parent/child environment (I talk/you listen).

➤ *Phase II: Compare and discuss worksheets.* Jim began comparing scores by focusing on areas of agreement. Then he moved to areas of disagreement, focusing first on areas where Joanne had underrated herself. Finally, he progressed to areas of disagreement where he felt that Joanne had not come to grips with a shortcoming. In most conversations, but especially when conducting performance appraisals, workleaders proceed from the positive end of the spectrum.

➤ *Phase III: Reinforce the scores.* Jim reviewed the scores to reinforce the results of the discussion. Pause at key items to offer guidance or clarify your or your associate's position. During this process workleaders use certain techniques to underscore the importance of the evaluation. They refer consistently to the worksheet in order to set the meeting's professional tone and purpose. If the conversation moves into touchy areas, the instrument can help neutralize emotion. Asking questions helps to direct the learning process and encourage personal responsibility.

➤ Using Evaluation as a Magnet of Positivism — Larry's Story

Leaders in organizational life today face few challenges greater than creating a sense of shared purpose among stakeholders. A key element in meeting this challenge is developing a set of ground rules and expectations that everyone can live by. Larry Anderson, one of our exceptional leaders and CEO of Excel Services, a multistate personnel placement and contract services firm, met the challenge masterfully.

"The bottom line," says Larry, "is the hypocrisy factor—agreeing to one set of standards one place and another set someplace else. We learned that you have to stand for the same thing regardless of the customer you serve, the challenge you face, or the number of people involved. It doesn't matter whether it's one person, a small team, or several thousand employees in the whole organization, what you stand for and the standards you put forth must be the same."

A classic entrepreneur, Larry grew up in a small town in the Midwest. After college he worked for several years in the banking field, where he first learned about personnel contract services. Approaching family and friends, including his former high school English teacher and scoutmaster, he raised $100,000 to start his own placement agency, promising his investors all his blood, sweat, and tears—plus a 100 percent return on their investment within five years. In just over seven years, the return hit 400 percent and is still climbing. In the field of contract personnel firms, where here today and gone tomorrow often applies, he has demonstrated an unrivaled resolve and integrity that has led to an astonishing 80 percent client retention.

Excel serves over 400 different client organizations engaged in virtually every type of business, healthcare, and governmental activity. To bring coherence to both his and his clients' needs, Larry conducts performance appraisals according to a very carefully organized schedule which incorporates the five key principles and the Performance Appraisal Worksheet. He applies his system to individual and team evaluations as well as to the organizations he serves. His approach helps him and his team measure their effectiveness systematically and provides everyone with the objective input they need to make course corrections before problems get out of hand.

Excel conducts performance appraisals of new staff every week during the first six weeks, as-needed for the next six weeks, and then regularly every 90 days. As Larry observes, "It is critically important to establish a positive, open attitude to performance appraisal early on in a relationship. We need newcomers to know that we live by the law of self-improvement and the only way you improve is through assessment."

Larry uses the same script format for both new and established staff who participate in brief quarterly reviews and an extensive review on their anniversary. "We see remarkable improvement by periodically keying into our associates and evaluating what's happening in their lives. We've turned away from a rather passive, laissez-faire leadership style to a highly involved and empowered strategy. The result is that all of us have become both more demanding and more tolerant. Because we better understand what's important, we spend less time worrying over inconsequential things."

The following excerpt of an evaluation session Larry led with his senior leadership team shows how everyone compared their perceptions of the organizational leadership team's effectiveness with customers' and employees' perceptions of the organization's overall performance.

Larry: As you know, we now have customer and employee evaluations in hand. We asked both groups to evaluate the overall effectiveness of our organization the same way we evaluate individual performance. Since we hold overall fiduciary responsibility for the welfare of both our customers and employees (*he reinforces organizational purpose*), I thought it would be interesting to compare our evaluation against those of the people we serve (*reinforces responsibility and involvement*). Let's follow the same process we do with our colleagues. Where are the areas of agreement and disagreement, strengths and weaknesses? Ann, why don't you walk us through the worksheet. *(Larry's organizational worksheet contains columns for customers' and associates' perspectives as well as a column for this leadership team's perspective. He guides the team by positively reinforcing responsibility and involvement.)*

Ann: Well, Larry, the first thing I notice is the general similarity between our scores and those of our customers for individual, team, and stewardship skills, though we *do* have a bit of a higher perception of ourselves than they do.

Joe: That's what struck me too, Larry. The differences with our employees also popped out, which really concerns me.

Larry: I understand how you feel Joe, but let's stick with the agenda. Where else do we see *positive* similarities? *(Larry affirms the discrepancy but pulls Joe back on line, sticking to the protocol of positive reinforcement first.)*

Beth: Well, I see one that's worth mentioning, information sharing. Customers, workers, and leadership all seem to agree that there is a good deal of openness. That's very encouraging and up two points from a year ago.

Joe: Yeah. That's important, but it doesn't seem to have pulled up the employee score much.

Ann: Come on, Joe, let's focus on the positive first and reinforce our strengths. Look at it from our customers' perspective. I think that eight for information sharing argues well for moving scores up overall in the near future.

Larry: Thanks for reminding me, Ann—that's positive reinforcement itself. But don't worry, Joe—we

Larry's Organizational Performance Appraisal Worksheet
Summary of Scores for Customers, Associates and the Leadership

Scoring
1 = Low   10 = High

Directions: Indicate the extent to which the organization demonstrates the following service skills.

	Customers	Associates	Leadership Team
I. Individual Customer Service Skills			
• Responsibility—provides ethical service, does not allow personal or organizational issues to interfere with fulfillment of customer needs	8	6	8
• Timeliness—provides responsive service	6	6	7
• Sensitivity—provides emotional support and understanding	7	4	8
• Accuracy—demonstrates clear comprehension of needs	8	7	8
• Coordination—provides service in the right sequence	5	5	5
• Thoroughness—meets the full range of customer needs	7	4	9
AVERAGE SCORE:	7	5	7.3
II. Team Service Skills			
• Respect and courtesy (Contact)	8	7	8
• Awareness of others' needs (Awareness)	7	5	7
• Willingness to become involved (Involvement)	6	5	9
• Empathy and understanding of others' needs (Empathy)	7	6	7
• Willingness to share information (Empowerment)	8	8	8
• Follow-through on work responsibilities (Commitment)	7	6	8
AVERAGE SCORE:	7	6	7.3
III. Stewardship Skills			
• Is present and punctual	8	7	8
• Utilizes financial and material resources efficiently	6	5	7
AVERAGE SCORE:	7	6	7.3
IV. Technical Service Skills **AVERAGE SCORE:**	7	8	9
(Total scores for each section and divide by 4) TOTAL SCORE:	7	6	8

V. Comments

VI. Improvement Contract

VII. Signatures _____   _____

won't sweep any important issues under the rug. *(Larry reinforces the whole team by affirming both Ann and Joe, so that a potential rift doesn't develop. He keeps the group focused on mining the areas where views of customers, leadership, and employees converge, and notes that they also all agreed that coordination needs measurable improvement, which leads to a suggestion from Beth.)*

Beth: Look, I think the coordination issue pretty obviously needs attention. I recommend we form a cross functional team of workers from different areas to identify the specific systems' breakdowns and make recommendations. I'll volunteer to advise, if no one else wants it.

Ann: I agree that's a real need, but can we hold off making a final decision until we address the gap between us and our employees?

Joe: Yeah. I agree. Now can I talk?

Larry: Sure Joe. But let me point out that we have found some very positive but cautious signs of hope, and that Beth has given us a good recommendation to come back to. Okay, Joe, go for it! Where do you see areas of disagreement? *(Larry reaffirms the connections with the team while reasserting the evaluation agenda. Then he invites Joe to proceed with the next step.)*

Larry used the evaluation protocol to stimulate a problem and opportunity discussion that set the stage for the development of a performance improvement contract with his leadership team. Throughout the meeting, he reinforced the five principles of evaluation by emphasizing purpose, responsibility, and involvement, and used a strategy of teaching and guiding to keep the team positively focused on evaluation as an opportunity for growth rather than a report card on failure. In addition to coordination, the team identified a need for improvement in several areas, including team courtesy and awareness and financial stewardship. They used this information and their commitment to each other to launch a problem-solving program for which they organized teams and made specific arrangements.

Larry, like other workleaders, has become a virtuoso at using the various roles and scripts in harmony: "I look at the workleader roles as Lego blocks to be used to build all kinds of customer-focused ways to succeed."

▇ FULFILLING THE ROLE OF THE EVALUATOR

Gandhi, Alicia, Jim, Val, and Larry demonstrate the power of positive evaluation, a process that strengthens the organization from the bottom up. As our research revealed, effective evaluation begins as an act of strategic humility whereby strong and competent individuals commit themselves to continuous improvement.

This commitment springs from a central commitment to the customer, whose needs define performance criteria for individuals, teams, and organizations. Two tools, the Key Principles of Effective Evaluation and the Performance Appraisal Worksheet, apply these criteria to all stakeholders and drive a collaborative five-phase interview process that produces a blueprint for continuous improvement.

Most important, as workleaders carry out the role of the evaluator they create a magnet of positivism—a belief in the perfectibility of people and organizations. This magnet exerts a powerful force for achievement. It attracts and strengthens the commitment of those determined to live work lives of substance and builds a reservoir of resolve to propel the system forward and negotiate new relationships, as we see in the next chapter.

6

The Negotiator

In the early afternoon of June 25, 1876, Lieutenant Colonel George Armstrong Custer led four companies of the U.S. Seventh Cavalry on a mission that has come to epitomize the disastrous consequences of pride and arrogance: Custer's Last Stand. The Sioux victory at the Little Big Horn saved a people from immediate genocide at the hands of the U.S. Cavalry and Indian Commissioners. That day's triumph was the result of a consummate act of negotiation—not a negotiation of surrender, but a negotiation which mobilized the spiritual and physical resources of a people.

By the winter of 1876, the 16,000 people of the Grand Teton Sioux nation, including the Hungkpapa, Minneconjou, Oglala, Sans Arc, Brule, and Black Feet tribes, and their close allies the Cheyenne, finally understood that they must unite or die. For more than twenty years Sitting Bull, the chief of chiefs and spiritual leader of the Hungkpapa, had urged greater unification of the tribes to confront the Blue Coat cavalry, miners, and settlers sent by the Great White Fathers in the East to steal the land and kill Ta Tanka, the buffalo. Though the tribes had won a major battle on the Bismarck trail in 1862, they had not consolidated their victory or leveraged their strength through unification. Instead they had returned to their old ways, searching the great sea of grass for buffalo as independent nomadic bands.

Sitting Bull knew that the Blue Coats would be back and that with them would come legions of their people. He urged the factions of the Grand Teton Sioux to unify and began a concerted effort to negotiate alliances. He was rebuffed at every turn until 1874, when miners under the protection of Custer's Seventh Cavalry found gold in the sacred Black Hills of Dakota. By that time the course of abuse, humiliation, and genocide had become too obvious to deny.

When federal agents came in 1875 to negotiate a purchase of the Black Hills, Sitting Bull recounted a list of crimes and broken treaties inflicted on his people. He picked up a pinch of earth and declared that he would not give up "even this much" of the Black Hills to such murderous people. Recognizing that this stand would precipitate a massive military response, Sitting Bull renewed his efforts to unify the Sioux tribes. Ironically, opposition again came from the once-proud tribal leaders of the 1860s. Back then, they had disdained alliance as unnecessary. Now, in 1875, they believed alliance was futile. Red Cloud, the great chief of chiefs during the Bismarck campaign, was despondent over the small pox and starvation raging through his Oglala band. He opposed unified resistance as hopeless and urged others to capitulate or die. Sitting Bull realized that just the opposite path of action was the key to survival. You cannot, he said, negotiate with a predator by offering him your children for dinner.

Recognizing the need to move beyond the established order of older chiefs, Sitting Bull initiated contact with a new generation of emerging leaders. He tuned into their individual needs and framed the challenge in terms they could understand and agree with. He approached Four Horns of the Brules and appealed to his well-known sense of social justice. What kind of people would destroy human life so wantonly and dishonorably? Surely, such people must be taught a lesson.

To Gall, his adopted cousin whose skill at hand-to-hand combat made him a most feared warrior in close-quarter battle, Sitting Bull spoke in terms of personal mastery. "Will you allow others to take control of your destiny, will you give up control to those who will destroy your women and children?" Little did Sitting Bull realize how ironic and prophetic were his questions. Gall would lose his wife and two of his children at the Little Big Horn.

He asked Crazy Horse, the greatest cavalry strategist of his day, "Will you stand by and watch the visions of your fathers and fathers' fathers destroyed?" And he asked all of the Sioux, "Will we forsake the heritage of our fathers to die like craven beasts, without honor and a home?"

Sitting Bull's genius was his ability to achieve consensus among the most historically independent and disconnected people in North America. He did not seek compromise among the tribes, which would have chipped away at the strength of each in tit-for-tat tradeoffs. Rather, he sought consensus for a solution that none of them could have achieved alone. For years Sitting Bull nurtured, cajoled, questioned, and probed his people to a state of readiness and awareness. He finally succeeded during the winter Feast of Making Fat held in the Black Hills in February of 1876. There, he consummated his negotiations with Four Horns, Gall, Crazy Horse, and others by issuing a call for all the Sioux peoples to meet in the sacred land of the Greasy Grass—the Little Big Horn—to honor the legacy of their ancestors. It was an invitation all were honor-bound to accept—and a threat the Blue Coats could not ignore.

Through relentless negotiation, Sitting Bull had found a solution to the problem of tribal disconnection. At the Little Big Horn the U.S. military suffered its most one-sided defeat in history at the hands of the largest recorded gathering of Native American warriors. This gave the U.S. government pause and gave Native American peoples a window of opportunity to forestall federal aggression. While continued trials lay ahead, Sitting Bull had negotiated a future for his people—not by selling out to his adversaries, but by harnessing the resources of his people to achieve a synergistic projection of will. Today his people still speak of him in the present tense, as a person of great heart whose commitment infuses their lives with hope.

■ THE ROLE OF THE NEGOTIATOR

The role of the negotiator is to achieve consensus on what needs to be done in order to serve the customer. Great negotiators create solutions more powerful and effective than anything that parties to the negotiation could have achieved individually. They achieve results by following two core principles. First, they negotiate for the customer, not for themselves. This is not an act of naive altruism, but a realization that greater personal achievement—even survival in the case of leaders like Sitting Bull—lies in achieving a collective vision.

This customer-first priority flies in the face of many popular notions that propose negotiating-to-win as a core strategy. The workleaders in our study were especially vocal on this issue. Andrew Spellman, a self-made millionaire sales representative for computer systems, explains: "The whole concept of winning through negotiation misses the point. If I win, you win, or even if we both win, the emphasis is on me and you, not on what's best for the people we both serve. Negotiation done in the framework of winning is always egocentric. When you negotiate to find a better way to serve, you build something greater than you could have accomplished by simply going for the win." Richard Muscatello, a seasoned collective bargaining negotiator, adds: "Sometimes, I even have to help the parties I'm negotiating with understand that what they want might not be in the best interests of the people they're representing and the customers on whom we all must rely. If we negotiate an agreement that serves our interests but not the customers', we will all lose our jobs."

Sitting Bull would never have been able to mobilize the Sioux if he had pursued a win for himself or even for a collection of the chiefs. He was finally able to break through to Crazy Horse when he challenged him to examine his motives. Driven by revenge for the deaths of his wife and daughter, Crazy Horse sought personal redemption in battle. Sitting Bull called his motives into question and challenged him to fight for more than self-interest: "You dishonor their memories if you fight for personal glory and not for your people."

To serve the customer, workleaders also seek to achieve consensus; this is the second core principle of negotiation. Consensus is very different from compromise. Compromise is based on the concept of *least losses*, or how to lose as little as possible. In a compromise, if I give something up you must do the same. The negotiations between the UAW and the big three automakers in the mid-70s provide an example of compromise. Facing the growing threat of Japanese competition, each compromised in ways that undermined their best interests, leaving them weaker, bitter, and unwilling to invest in each other. Their compromise agreement delayed an effective American response to global competition by nearly a decade.

By contrast, consensus is the process of achieving synergy by combining the strengths and visions of each party in a new way to achieve something neither could have achieved alone. Like Sitting Bull, workleaders demonstrate the ability to transform negotiation into collaborative research efforts to find new and more potent formulas for success. Microsoft, for example, fueled its growth into an industry leader through consensus negotiation with its customers. Recognizing that early software left much to be desired, Microsoft developed a nationwide network of customer testing sites where buying customers were guaranteed free upgrades to critique and debug software. Both sides invested in the other to create one of the most rapid response research and development processes in history.

The combination of a customer-first priority plus consensus building methodology can achieve dramatic success, as demonstrated by two special studies we conducted. The first was a direct comparison of 147 workleaders in business-to-business sales with 342 average performers holding the same positions. Compared to average leaders, workleaders generated 27 percent higher sales volume, 35 percent higher profit margins, 71 percent higher levels of customer satisfaction, and 53 percent higher levels of customer retention. A second study of 43 workleaders and 65 average leaders involved in labor negotiations found that workleaders concluded their negotiations in 25 percent less time than average leaders for wage increases that were 5 percent lower. Most importantly, negotiators representing labor interests reported 40 percent higher levels of trust and satisfaction with workleaders than with average leaders.

These results and those achieved by Sitting Bull and Microsoft demonstrate the power of defining the role of the negotiator by the principles of customer service and consensus building: The negotiator serves the customer by achieving consensus on what needs to be done. To fulfill this role, workleaders carry out two specific functions. First, they diagnose customer needs in order to understand the issues and concerns that must be addressed to reach consensus. Second, this enables them to move negotiations along a path to consensus through a carefully designed communication strategy of questions.

We have organized the way in which workleaders perform these functions into two tools, the *Customer Needs Analyzer* and the *Consensus Negotiating Guide*. Before applying each tool, consider the following overview of the role of the negotiator (see chart).

➤ Tool #1: The Customer Needs Analyzer

Workleaders concurrently analyze customer needs and move along the path to consensus. However, we have found it useful in our workshops to examine each function separately

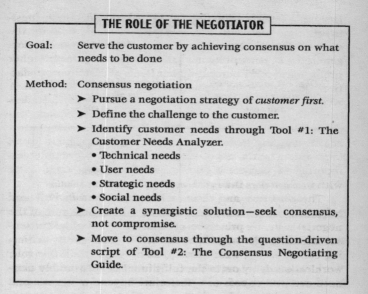

THE ROLE OF THE NEGOTIATOR

Goal: Serve the customer by achieving consensus on what needs to be done

Method: Consensus negotiation
➤ Pursue a negotiation strategy of *customer first*.
➤ Define the challenge to the customer.
➤ Identify customer needs through Tool #1: The Customer Needs Analyzer.
 • Technical needs
 • User needs
 • Strategic needs
 • Social needs
➤ Create a synergistic solution—seek consensus, not compromise.
➤ Move to consensus through the question-driven script of Tool #2: The Consensus Negotiating Guide.

before combining them in a comprehensive case study. An analysis of the customer needs addressed in workleader negotiations revealed four core categories. Intriguingly, these needs are essentially the same regardless of the issue of the negotiations, from sales to collective bargaining to individual employment. They include the technical, user, strategic, and social needs which are illustrated in the Customer Needs Analyzer grid. Analyzing these needs helps workleaders develop communication strategies for educating, problem solving, and finding solutions to negotiation challenges. By identifying customer needs, workleaders are able to develop finely tuned consensus building techniques for negotiating solutions. Let's define each of the customer needs and see how they can be identified through targeted needs analysis scripts.

```
┌──────────────────────────────────────────────┐
│              THE CUSTOMER NEEDS ANALYZER       │
├────────────────────────┬───────────────────────┤
│   Technical Needs      │    Strategic Needs     │
│                        │                        │
│     At issue:          │      At issue:         │
│  Does the solution meet│  How will the solution │
│ specifications for     │    take us where we    │
│  performance and cost? │        need to go?     │
├────────────────────────┼───────────────────────┤
│     User Needs         │     Social Needs       │
│                        │                        │
│     At issue:          │      At issue:         │
│  How will the solution │   How will the solution│
│     work for me?       │   support the culture? │
└────────────────────────┴───────────────────────┘
```

Technical Needs

Technical needs relate to the fulfillment of measurable performance and cost issues. Technical buyers or negotiators serve as gatekeepers in negotiations: Their role is to use technicalities to screen out proposed solutions. Their input is based on a variety of specifications that may or may not be technical but can be framed in quantifiable terms. In sales negotiations, for example, purchasing agents and financial managers can act as gatekeepers and screen out prospective vendors by raising issues of price, logistics, references, and technical performance specifications. They can halt negotiations even when there is an otherwise seemingly perfect match between a product and service and a company's needs. In collective bargaining, for example, a union attorney can act as a technical buyer by raising concerns related to contractual and financial issues.

Knowledge of the customer's technical needs is essential to developing a negotiating solution. Workleaders attempt to identify technical needs early on in the negotiating process. The earlier they know a customer's technical needs, the more discussion time they have to develop reasonable ways to address even needs that might seem unreasonable. The basic script strategy for identifying technical needs openly acknowledges their importance and the negotiator's willingness to address them.

A Script for Identifying Technical Needs

Betty Smith, a real estate agent, is negotiating a price with Tim Carland, who hopes to sell his house.

> **Betty:** Mr. Carland, I need to be sure I really understand your needs and requirements regarding price. May I ask, what's your bottom line? What must you get? *(Betty communicates her openness and willingness to address the important issues. She also clarifies her responsibility and that of her partner by asking a question.)*
>
> **Tim:** As much as we can. What do you think its value is on the market? *(Technical negotiators request data support—quantifiable information—for their decisions.)*
>
> **Betty:** Here's a market assessment we completed which includes the sale of a home just up the street. We believe yours should sell for about ten thousand dollars more because of size and condition. *(She provides physical data and also gives reasons he can understand for her assessment of his case.)*
>
> **Tim:** I see. Yes, that was the Goodson's house. This makes sense. May I have copies of the data?
>
> **Betty:** Of course. This set is for you.

Technical buyers need to feel in control of a situation, and they need quantifiable results to defend their position.

User Needs

User needs relate to the actual use of a product or service. Customers with user needs have direct operational service and production responsibilities, and need to know "Will this work for me? Will it help me achieve my individual performance goals and objectives?" Front-line workers and operational managers often have very specific, concrete needs for a product or service to help them meet their immediate challenges. Their needs are typically very complex and involve both such subjective, personal issues as job security and objective realities such as the everyday pressures of work performance. To meet user needs, a negotiator has to demonstrate a potentially direct link between a user's personal success and a specific solution.

A Script for Identifying User Needs

Betty has identified prospects for Tim Carland's house. She is speaking with Jean DiCenzo, a prospective buyer, about user needs.

Betty: Jean, I need to have an understanding of your day-to-day needs to identify houses for your consideration. What are your most important considerations? *(Again, Betty communicates her openness and clarifies her responsibility. She also demonstrates her willingness to address the negotiation in Jean's terms.)*

Jean: Safety and comfort. It has to be secure because the kids will be coming home from school before we return from work. And it has to be comfortable—it has to have a large kitchen and eating area. So preparing and serving dinner is no hassle.

Betty: Anything else?

Jean: Bathrooms! It must have a minimum of *two* upstairs—one for the kids and one for Mark and me. The rush in the morning can make you crazy if you can't get in the bathroom.

User needs tend to be very practical on one hand but potentially emotional on the other, because the user is completely immersed in the realities of the solution in question. Users must feel that the negotiator is proposing something that will assist them in the work of day-to-day life.

Strategic Needs

Strategic needs relate to the benefits of a particular solution for the overall mission and welfare of an organization. Often senior members of organizations have strategic needs; people with strategic needs also tend to have direct influence over economic decisions related to negotiation and can select between divergent points of view. For example, if a financial controller says that a particular proposal appears to be too expensive but an operational manager says that it could improve customer satisfaction and profit margins, a strategist such as a general manager may provide the deciding vote and go with the proposal if it fits the organization's strategic vision. The strategic negotiator thinks in terms of potential return on investment as measured by a proposal's ability to meet such strategic goals as overall organizational strength, market share, and profits.

A Script for Identifying Strategic Needs

Betty needs to discuss strategic considerations regarding the purchase of a house with Jean and her husband Mark.

Betty: What is it that you ultimately want to get out of this home—your hopes and expectations? *(In order to discuss the subject in terms of strategic concerns, Betty phrases her question in terms of strategy. She also puts the onus on Jean and Mark to establish their priorities.)*

Mark: It must be a good long-term investment. We have to be sure that it has good appreciation potential and that the price we pay provides room for growth in the future sales price of the house.

Jean: I think we have to be sure it's in an area that will hold and increase value.

Mark: Yes, and one that has a good reputation for being progressive and taking the lead.

Strategic needs define the buyer or negotiator's long-term view. They help explain how a particular solution fits into a larger life plan for either individuals or organizations.

Social Needs

Social needs relate to cultural issues of values and interpersonal relationships. For a negotiator concerned with social needs, the question is "How will this solution impact the quality of life of our customers and those who serve the customer, and what will this solution mean to our commitments to people and our ability to project our mission into the future?" An example of a social needs negotiator would be the vice president of mission for a religiously affiliated hospital who wants to know how a solution can protect the hospital's ability to serve the poor. Another example would be the president of a local union who wants to know how a solution can protect the jobs of people with whom she has worked side by side. Still another example would be the founder of a corporation facing a merger offer who wants to know how the buyout will protect the company's reputation.

A *Script for Identifying Social Needs*

Betty asks Jean and Mark about social needs related to the purchase of a home, especially concerns related to their children.

> *Betty:* Are there any special social needs that you want me to consider? Jean, you mentioned children— what about them? *(Again, Betty leaves the question open-ended in order to ensure that Jean and Mark's answer reflects how they feel about the issue and that the responsibility for their answer rests with them.)*

> *Jean:* Alison is a sophomore in high school and Tad is in seventh grade. My concern is that the schools offer good opportunities for them to get involved in extracurricular activities. Alison will always make her way, but Tad needs some specific opportunities like swimming and band.

> *Mark:* And it's important that there's an active community and church life available as well. We need to feel we really belong. Though I don't have a lot of time, I'd like to get involved in one of the service organizations.

An understanding of social needs is essential to evaluate a proposed solution's overall suitability. Social needs are more difficult to define than technical, user, and strategic needs because they are more personal and therefore more closely guarded by the parties involved in a negotiation. They usually emerge last in a needs analysis.

➤ Tool #2: The Consensus Negotiating Guide

In their negotiations workleaders demonstrate an extraordinary ability to develop mutual ownership of challenges with negotiating partners. Such ownership is essential to tap the full potential of others, which is in turn essential to develop and implement new and creative decisions. The process workleaders employ to achieve joint ownership is *consensus negotiation* and its driving strategy is a blueprint of consensus-building questions. These questions are designed to achieve consensus on specific objectives at every stage of negotiation. Like locks in a canal, a new and higher level of consensus is achieved as each objective is reached. By the time the parties face the seventh and final objective, only a short distance remains to the high water level.

Workleaders have developed the capacity to tune in, reframe, redirect, and tie down agreement through an array of very specific questions. As with the needs analysis, these questions are essentially universal regardless of the type of negotiation, from sales to collective bargaining to merger discussions. Negotiation is a universal function that forms a key part of just about every aspect of a workleader's life.

The Consensus Negotiation Guide is a summary of this blueprint. The types of questions it presents are designed to build consensus on seven specific objectives. Accord must be reached on all seven in order to achieve full consensus. First of all, for a negotiation to be successful there must be consensus regarding its purpose. Agreement on a negotiation's purpose provides a base from which a variety of modulations can be explored. It's very much like jazz variations on a melody. Once the melody is firmly fixed in our minds, we welcome the creative exploration of its full potential. Workleaders insist on a clear statement of the melodic purpose for negotiation by asking such questions as "Is this the real challenge?" and then rephrasing the challenge in the words of the negotiating partner: "I see, as you've said, our

most important objective is to achieve X, correct?" Such probing and paraphrasing is continued until the response is *yes*.

This simple *yes* response frames the discussion positively
and makes it possible to pursue the second objective: Identify specific customer needs. As discussed previously, these
are technical, user, strategic, and social needs. They are identified through a very direct and uncomplicated process of
explaining the reasons for inquiring about the negotiating
party's needs: "In the context of our challenge, it would be
very helpful for me to know what needs you believe we must
absolutely address. Do you think we need data, information
on how things work, a projection of the long-term value of
the solution we might develop, or a sense of people's personal reactions to it?"

Such questions are designed to provide options. Our
workleaders intuitively understand cognitive scientists' findings that it is easier to answer when you have something to
choose from or react to. A negotiator is also more likely to
get a useful response and direct a conversation by asking a
question that offers options. Workleaders demonstrate both
courtesy and savvy by asking questions that help point their
partners in the direction they need to go.

Consensus on needs sets the stage to build consensus
regarding the need to work cooperatively. At this stage the
negotiation matures from a vague agreement to work together to an explicit commitment. Workleaders are especially effective in moving negotiations to this stage by
simply asking permission to seek a solution together: "Now
that we've done some of the hardest work by defining the
overall challenge and specific needs to be met, we can really
begin to make progress. With your permission, I'd like to
develop some solutions for your consideration and reaction.
Agreed?"

As solutions are developed, test them by exploring various ways in which they could be implemented. "What if we
tried this . . . ?" is a standard question that frames the solu-

tion as an option for collaborative problem solving. This technique has the special benefit of developing ownership for a solution through shared decision making. Without having to make a final commitment, both parties engage in the heart of negotiation by developing the substance of an agreement. This is the stage at which the deal is actually struck—and the way is paved for a serious discussion of implementation, including the identification of objections and barriers that might be thrown in the way.

"What are the fears and feelings that could get in the way of this solution?" is the question at the next stage. The fear of being rejected, looking stupid, or losing power are potential barriers in any negotiation. Probe for these fears by asking questions designed to clarify the feelings and needs of those who will be affected by the proposed solution. These questions examine the extent to which earlier analysis is accurate and complete. They provide data for fine-tuning the solution and tying down an agreement to take action: "Now that we've redesigned things to overcome Harvey's fears, *don't you think we should* get this signed and get started so we can meet our schedule?" *Don't you, shouldn't we, can't we, haven't they* and *doesn't it* are the beginnings of tie-down questions that bring negotiation to a stage of consensus and action.

Let's analyze a labor negotiation discussion between a workleader and a union representative to see how this blueprint for negotiation might work.

➤ A Script for Consensus Negotiations in Collective Bargaining

Dana is a seasoned workleader charged with responsibility for resolving some final questions that are holding up a collective bargaining agreement. She meets with Mike, president of the local union, to move things to consensus.

TOOL #2: THE CONSENSUS NEGOTIATING GUIDE

Stage I: Establish purpose.

Objective 1: Build consensus on the purpose for negotiation.

Strategy 1:   Ask challenge clarification questions.
Ask follow-up paraphrasing questions to build consensus on the objective.

Stage II: Identify customer needs.

Objective 2: • Build consensus on specific customer needs.

Strategy 2:   • Ask technical, user, strategic, and social needs clarification questions.

Stage III: Develop a solution.

Objective 3: • Build consensus on the need to develop a solution.

Strategy 3:   • Ask permission to problem solve together.

Stage IV: Test the solution.

Objective 4: • Build consensus on how to sell the solution.

Strategy 4:   • Test the solution through *what if* questions.

Stage V: Identify barriers.

Objective 5: • Build consensus on possible barriers to consensus.

Strategy 5:   • Ask *what do you suppose* questions to root out fear, low esteem, and pride.

Stage VI: Overcome barriers.

Objective 6: • Build consensus on how to overcome barriers and objectives.

Strategy 6:   • Ask reframing questions that build positive expectations.

Stage VII: Take action together.

Objective 7: • Achieve consensus on what to do.

Strategy 7:   • Ask tie-down questions.

Dana: Mike, thank you for the opportunity to meet to address our remaining challenges. May I ask you for your analysis of where we stand and what our objective should be here today? *(Dana establishes contact through courtesy, frames the issue for negotiation, and then asks Mike a clarifying question.)*

Mike: Well, Dana, the challenge, frankly, is explaining to my people why they should agree to anything when they don't know what management's plans are for the future. If we sign a three-year agreement and you all sell the business, then where are we?

Dana: Oh, I understand. You're saying that your people don't know why they should agree to a plan for their future when they don't know a major piece of the plan—namely, the future for the business as a whole. Is that right? *(Dana paraphrases and asks for agreement.)*

Mike: Yeah, more or less.

Dana: Then our objective or challenge here today is to figure out how to provide them with the information they need to make a decision. Right? *(Dana continues to seek clarification, moving Mike along the path to consensus by offering him increasingly specific options for agreement.)*

Mike: Yes, but I think they want more than a plan—they want a promise, a promise of job security.

Dana: Mike, I understand they *want* job security—so do I—but do they *need* a guarantee of job security, or do they need reliable information on what is likely to happen to this business and all of our futures? *(Dana accepts Mike's yes to the challenge, moves directly to Stage II, and probes for specific user needs.)*

Mike: Well, certainly reliable information, yes. They do know there are no promises for anyone anymore, but it's hard to take.

Dana: It's especially hard to take for our customers. That's why we've been working so hard on building good relationships with you and your people. Our customers need and deserve our full attention, not our anxiety. Let me see if I've got this straight. Your people need reliable information on where we're going, as best as we can see it today. They need to see tangible evidence of why they should go ahead with the agreement. They need to see that some forethought, planning, and commitment have gone into our future. They want evidence of our sincerity, not our good wishes. Right? *(Dana takes the opportunity to frame the negotiations in terms of the larger standard to which they all must hold themselves accountable, linking union members' needs to those of the customer. Then she zeroes in to clarify and reach consensus on the technical information needs Mike has to fulfill.)*

Mike: Right.

Dana: And that's what you have got to bring back. Otherwise, they'll wonder what's going on in these discussions. Right? *(Dana probes more deeply to clarify Mike's personal needs. She realizes that the union members' need for information creates user and social needs for Mike. He has to demonstrate his competency and commitment by bringing back results.)*

Mike: Well . . . to be truthful, yes. Just like you, I have to prove my worth to my customers—my members.

Dana: I understand that need very clearly. Mike, it seems to me we need to think this through together. I think I've got a solution but I'd like to ask if it would be all right to develop it together. *(Dana moves to Stage III to seek consensus on joint problem solving.)*

Mike: Well, of course it depends on whether it serves my people's interests.

Dana: It serves all of our interests and, more importantly, the customers'. Our executive team and the board have been developing a strategic plan for expanding this company and, if you agree, I'm going to get permission to share the majority of it with you so we can develop the information you need to bring back. Will you work with me on it if I get permission? *(Dana senses an opportunity to push ahead and proposes the beginnings of a solution to give Mike the option of deciding whether to give permission to collaborate.)*

Mike: Yeah. That's what they need—and I need. We can't stay out of the loop any longer.

Dana: Of course you can't. I'm virtually certain I'll get permission to share most of the plan—we've already talked about conducting town hall meetings with employees. What if we meet tomorrow to begin work, and you report to your people that we're moving forward on getting them what they need. And what if we set a two week schedule to get you information to report back? How does that plan sound?

Mike: It sounds pretty good. *(Dana moves to Stage IV and tests through* what if *questions.)*

Dana: Well, if we delivered information back and ran town halls explaining the future, would there be any reason that we can't wrap this agreement up in six weeks as scheduled? What do you suppose could stop us? *(Dana presses the transition to Stage V, barrier identification, in order to maintain momentum and probe for objections and opposition.)*

Mike: Well, maybe fate and a history of being kept in the dark.

Dana: Mike, I understand the history, but you and I have brought it this far because we've developed an open and trusting relationship. Can't we do the same here? Can't we use our sessions together in some way to set the stage for agreement? Perhaps you could have some of your people join you in our meetings, once we get going? *(Dana moves to Stage VI and confronts the barriers by fine-tuning their solution to include others in the meetings. She reframes the discussion from the slight negative downturn marked by Mike's concerns to a reaffirmation of their commitment.)*

Mike: Dana, that's probably the answer. That way there's no question about what information was discussed or shared. It protects me and you.

Dana: I agree, Mike. Why don't we shake on it and agree to meet tomorrow at the same time and place. *(Dana moves directly to the tie-down at Stage VII.)*

Mike: Agreed.

In this scenario, Dana followed the seven-step consensus negotiation protocol to address a testy challenge that cropped up during a labor negotiation. Workleaders use the seven-step process both to frame the larger strategy and to deal with specific interactions. In the next case study we see how Walt Diesing uses the consensus negotiation process to close a sales negotiation.

➤ Getting to Consensus — Walt's Story

Walt Diesing, like Sitting Bull, Dana, and our other workleaders, has achieved a remarkable history of accomplishment. He started his own computer systems consulting firm after working 12 years as senior programmer and then vice president of information services for a large retail department store chain. He decided to leave when the part-time requests for help he'd been handling grew to take almost as much time as his full-time job. He loved negotiating solutions to special challenges and his reputation as an honest and conscientious systems designer caught the attention of people at Holiday Pools.

Walt Diesing has been working on the sale of a comprehensive computerized customer service management system for Holiday Pools, including new client applications software for word processing, spreadsheets, graphics, and network management software and hardware for a 20-station PC server network. Walt has worked hard to provide this rapidly growing and soon to be franchised store a state-of-the-art but cost-efficient system that can be replicated nationwide as the company grows. He feels he's very near consensus with all the significant parties, but a few hurdles remain. Walt has utilized the Customer Needs Analyzer to profile the individuals he will be meeting with and uses the Consensus Negotiating Guide to move the different stages of conversations to consensus.

Walt starts what he hopes will be his final round of negotiations with the executive team of Holiday Pools. He's asked for a few minutes with Tamarra, the president and CEO, before the rest of the team joins them. A former Miss America runner-up and swimming champion, she has been a remarkable visionary. Walt picks up the conversation where he left it last week, testing solutions he has designed to key into specific needs.

Walt: Tamarra, thanks for taking a few minutes to meet with me before our team review.

WALT'S CUSTOMER NEEDS ANALYZER	
Technical Buyer: Meredith *Does it meet specs?* *What are the costs?*	Strategic Buyer: Tamarra *How will this take us* *where we need to go?*
User Buyer: Ethel *How will it work for me?*	Social Buyer: Abe *How will it support our people?*

Tamarra: It's always a pleasure to see you, Walt. What's up?

Walt: I wanted to clarify your thoughts on how important it would be for you to be able to expand this system. What if you opened several stores next year? *(Walt reestablishes contact at Stage IV to reinforce the consensus that he and Tamarra had reached.)*

Tamarra: Well, as we discussed, that's exactly what we are going to do. And it's absolutely essential that this system is able to grow to handle it. That's been a strategic requirement from the beginning. We've raised the money to grow, and grow we will.

Walt: I hear you loud and clear. I've designed the system to be expandable. I'm just wondering if anything could come up that would be a barrier to going forward. *(Walt reinforces their consensus to provide a base from which to move to Stage V and identify objections. He wants to make sure there are no likely surprises ahead in the team meeting.)*

Tamarra:	Well, Meredith is, as always, rightly concerned with costs. And Ethel is concerned that it won't do the job, while Abe—well, Abe is just concerned. It's a big change from the mom-and-pop culture we've run.
Walt:	Their concerns are perfectly understandable and I just wanted to ask you: If we're able to handle their concerns, would you want to take action immediately, or wait two to three weeks? *(Walt reframes the negotiation to establish a positive set of expectations for moving forward—Stage VI, providing options in order to make it easier to respond.)*
Tamarra:	Walt, this needs to move forward now if at all possible. But let's see where the team is on this. Here they come now. *(As the team convenes, Walt greets each individually and waits for Tamarra to open the discussion. Walt has reconfirmed his consensus with Tamarra. He realizes that each team member has new concerns that need to be addressed based on review of the proposal that Walt submitted to them for discussion two weeks ago.)* Good afternoon, everyone. We're here to pick up our discussions with Walt. Walt, why don't I ask you to guide us through the discussion?
Walt:	Thank you. Well, we've come a long way in our discussions. We've identified a significant challenge to manage information, to improve customer service, to equip the company to expand and grow, and to do all of this cost effectively and with sensitivity to the people who have to do the job. And together we've developed a proposal to meet these challenges. Today, however, I realize we need to go to the next step in our discussions and

identify the remaining objections and barriers to moving forward. I'd like to ask each of you what concerns or barriers we still need to address. *(Walt begins by reviewing the stage-by-stage consensus they have reached together. This reinforces their existing investment in the solution and makes it clear that there is only a relatively short distance yet to go to reach full consensus. He asks a Stage V question to elicit the objections for which he has already prepared answers.)*

Meredith: Walt, I think the proposal is great, if we can afford it. I want to make sure the price is the best we can get.

Walt: I'm concerned too, Meredith. I want to make sure this solution has legs as you grow. What I hear you saying is that you need a way to make absolutely sure the price we pay for the software and hardware is the best we can get, providing we get good and dependable service too. Is that accurate?

Meredith: Yes, exactly.

Walt: Well, recognizing the company's need to get the best price, I've prepared a list of several suppliers for each piece of software and hardware, with quotations for individual and systems purchases. Given the importance of this, I'd like to propose that one of your staff help to check those figures out, just to be sure we're doing the best we can. But do you think that would deal with the cost issue? *(Walt reframes the question to key into his needs and strengthen the consensus they have already built.)*

Meredith: Well, actually, it just might.

Walt:	And it also starts to build expertise for pricing equipment as the system grows, decreasing dependence on outsiders like me. Wouldn't you agree? Don't worry, I won't take offense. *(Walt uses tie-down questions— Stage V—to move Meredith towards consensus to act, providing her with options that fill her technical needs profile for control. The question is also directed toward Ethel. Collective problem solving—Stage IV—will recapture the consensus they had developed.)*
Meredith:	Walt, frankly, you're reading my mind. You know I have to protect stockholder equity, and this type of data and control helps. Yes, I agree.
Ethel:	Well, yes, that would certainly help. Could we include a couple of my staff in this, the people whose work lives will be most affected?
Walt:	Absolutely. And before we go, I've prepared a present. What if we could get hold of a library of various forms that other people developed on the system and use that to get our creative juices going?
Ethel:	Walt, stop teasing. Hand it over. You know that's what we want.
Walt:	Just for you, Ethel. Tell the team you made me work night and day for a week just to put it together. Don't you think that might convert them? *(Walt offers the solutions in two steps to get maximum impact and to set up the tie-down, Stage VII.)*
Ethel:	You're almost there, Walt. But we don't want to make this easy.

Abe: Don't worry, Ethel, I won't. Walt, my concern is the people. They're already a bit shell-shocked by the growth and wondering whether they'll be left behind.

Walt: That, too, is an absolutely critical concern, but one with a particularly positive solution. Abe, we can provide each person with a private tutorial on the system, including training on every phase of the customer service process. They'll be able to be cross-trained in how to work in virtually every role from order entry to shipping to customer problem solving. Do you think that will help address anxiety over the future? *(Walt affirms the importance of the challenge, agreeing with Abe and then, recognizing the momentum he's created with Tamarra, Meredith, and Ethel, moves from challenge clarification to tie-down, Stage VII, by proposing a powerful solution.)*

Abe: Very definitely. I didn't realize that kind of support was possible.

Walt: Well, there's even more available as we go forward. If it isn't too presumptuous, can I ask you all a question? If these solutions stand up on review, shouldn't we get going and move to implementation?

Tamarra: That's a fair question and deserves a fair answer. If they hold up, which we all know they will, I think I speak for all of us and would agree we need to move forward.

Walt used the Consensus Negotiation Guide to design an architecture of consensus in which every party to the decision could contribute to create a solution that none of them could have built alone. Walt, like our other workleaders, demonstrates the capacity to tune into the needs of others to develop ways to serve more effectively. In the process, he harnessed the resources of Holiday Pools to create a synergy of insight that helped them to break through to the next level of achievement.

■ FULFILLING THE ROLE OF THE NEGOTIATOR

The role of the negotiator is central to the effectiveness of every workleader. Whether a leader serves in production, direct customer service, labor relations management, strategic planning, or sales, the ability to achieve consensus for the customer is the key to success. Our research confirmed the extraordinary versatility of negotiation as an everyday tool to enrich the capacity to carry out other roles.

Negotiation expands the options for problem solving, provides an endgame for selection, expands the repertoire of the connector, reinforces the teaching effectiveness of the evaluator, and provides a positive complement to the incisive power of the healing role, the subject of our next chapter.

7

The Healer

On a cold November day in 1863 President Abraham Lincoln made a sorrowful journey to Gettysburg, Pennsylvania. Sitting alone in a private railway car, he pondered the fate of a nation that had been ripped apart by the Civil War and he weighed the words he would use to dedicate the National Cemetery on Cemetery Hill, the stark and final resting place of 3,629 slain soldiers, 1,630 of them unknown. As news of the battle at Gettysburg had come to Washington on July 3, 1863, President Lincoln knew that the tide of the war had finally turned. The defeat of the Confederacy now seemed inevitable. Far from rejoicing over the Union's victory, the President thought instead about the need to shift his focus from waging war to healing the wounds of a shattered nation.

How could he wrest renewal and hope from the devastation, humiliation, and tragedy of human suffering that had afflicted his people? While Lincoln had unreservedly and tenaciously prosecuted the war, he had done so with the overriding hope that he could renew the life of the nation and, as he said in his annual message to Congress on December 1, 1862, protect "the last, best hope of earth."

From the outset of his leadership career Lincoln spoke to "the better angels of our nature." Even in the midst of a viciously destructive war that took over a million lives and left untold millions destitute and homeless, Lincoln retained his faith in people and their responsiveness to the ideals of democracy and brotherhood, a mission to which he testified in his second Inaugural Address on March 4, 1865: "With malice towards none, with charity for all; with firmness in the right . . . let us strive on . . . to bind up the nation's wounds."

No American leader has ever faced a tangle of issues more difficult to sort out in morally convincing terms than did Lincoln. The industrial revolution had made it possible for soldiers to kill their fellow citizens with a terrible new efficacy, a fact borne out by the casualties at Gettysburg. During a three-day battle that began on July 2, 101,100 Union troops under General Meade clashed with 70,000 Confederate soldiers commanded by General Lee. When General Lee ordered a retreat under the cover of darkness on the night of July 4, the toll was astonishing: 28,000 Union and 23,000 Confederate casualties.

As Lincoln prepared his commemoration address, he faced a divided constituency even in the North—one that had not reached consensus over the constitutionality of secession, the morality of abolition, or the limits of compromise. In order to heal his nation, he knew he could not assume or assert unanimity on such issues, but somehow had to instead find basic points of agreement that transcended differences and brought people back together. Thus, he chose to stress the universality of suffering so painfully impressed on the nation's consciousness at Gettysburg. Those in attendance at the ceremony expected a lengthy speech, especially after listening to the keynote orator, Edward Everett, for over two hours. The brevity of Lincoln's remarks took everyone by surprise, but that three-minute speech has gone down in history as one of the most powerful addresses ever given:

We cannot dedicate—we cannot consecrate—we cannot hallow—this ground. The brave men, living and dead, who struggled here have consecrated it, far above our poor power to add or detract. The world will little note, nor long remember what we say here, but it can never forget what they did here. It is for us the living, rather, to be dedicated here to the unfinished work which they who fought here have thus far so nobly advanced. . . . that from these honored dead we take increased devotion to that cause for which they gave the last full measure of devotion—that we here highly resolve that these dead shall not have died in vain—that this nation, under God, shall have a new birth of freedom—and that government of the people, by the people, for the people, shall not perish from the earth.

—THE GETTYSBURG ADDRESS
November 19, 1863

Those words, as much as any divisive battle, marked the turning point of the war from a conflict that pitted brother against brother to a consensus that the human spirit must prosper even in the face of death and defeat.

■ THE ROLE OF THE HEALER

Like Lincoln, exceptional leaders today accept responsibility to appeal to "the better angels" of human nature. Though they encounter circumstances far less grave than those Lincoln addressed at Gettysburg, the costs of corporate restructuring and economic battles in the contemporary workplace have caused so much distrust and suffering that the numbers of "killed and wounded" continue to mount.

The workleaders in our study demonstrate a keen awareness of the cost of human suffering and an ability to reduce this cost by refocusing energies on the healing process. The statistics for attendance, wellness, and productivity for associates under workleaders' influence run remarkably higher than those under average leaders. Average leaders experience twice the rate of absenteeism and 53 percent higher levels of serious illnesses reported by workers, including heart disease, cancer, and emotional stress disorders; finally, as we report in the problem-solving and negotiation chapters (Chapters 4 and 6), average leaders record significantly lower levels of productivity and customer satisfaction. Lincoln understood that a divided nation is a sick nation; likewise contemporary leaders understand that a divided and distressed workforce is a sick workforce.

While workleaders demonstrate unexpectedly high levels of competence in skills typically associated with health professionals, they also maintain a firm grasp on their limits. They know how to diagnose the symptoms of organizational disease early on, and they intervene early to provide assistance and/or secure the necessary prescriptions for healing. At the same time, they display a strategic understanding of their role's limits, as illustrated by the comments of Rosemary Stafford, a psychiatric nurse manager: "It's critically important to know when you've slipped into *nursing,* not leading, your staff. In our business, there's a high risk that we will 'catch' a dose of the depression, anxiety, or dependence of our patients. I know the signs and try to intervene early to head them off. If the problem has progressed, however, I direct the staff member to outside help immediately. I need to remind myself of my limits and know that if I slip too far into the role of therapist I undermine my ability to protect the health of everyone."

Workleaders remain acutely aware of their responsibility to heal, and they know how to categorize problems as those that can be managed within the framework of daily work and those that require other assistance. To fulfill their role as healers, they diagnose the signs of distress which we've organized into Tool #1: The *Healing Needs Analyzer,* then take action with Tool #2: The *Healing Guide.* Before we proceed to a discussion of each tool, consider this summary of the role of the healer.

Healers follow the cardinal rule of medical intervention: First, do no harm. Avoid treating imaginary ailments and never prescribe solutions that do not match the specific con-

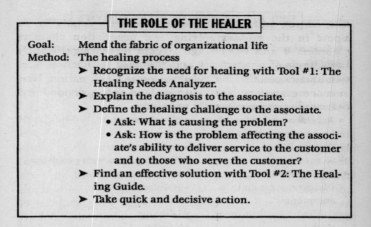

THE ROLE OF THE HEALER

Goal: Mend the fabric of organizational life
Method: The healing process
➤ Recognize the need for healing with Tool #1: The Healing Needs Analyzer.
➤ Explain the diagnosis to the associate.
➤ Define the healing challenge to the associate.
  • Ask: What is causing the problem?
  • Ask: How is the problem affecting the associate's ability to deliver service to the customer and to those who serve the customer?
➤ Find an effective solution with Tool #2: The Healing Guide.
➤ Take quick and decisive action.

dition. In order to pinpoint a real ailment, the healer produces a diagnostic protocol in much the same way a doctor would.

➤ Tool #1: The Healing Needs Analyzer

The Healing Needs Analyzer provides a diagnostic map of behavioral, attitudinal, and physical changes in performance that may signal the need for a healing intervention. As with the other tools in this book, workleaders employ this tool concurrently with the Healing Guide. However, we will first explore the diagnostic phase of the healing process.

A rule of thumb guides healers as they identify problems: They step in and find out what's going on when they observe three to five behavioral, attitudinal, or physical problems.

The following chart, which may vary from workleader to workleader, isolates the three key types of symptoms that can signal individual, team, and organizational health problems. Workleaders examine behaviors, attitudes, and physi-

TOOL #1: THE HEALING NEEDS ANALYZER

I. Behavioral indicators

- Not sharing
- Rushing around
- Poor organization
- Poor time management
- Aggressive behavior
- Poor concentration
- Forgetfulness
- Slow reaction
- Confused thinking
- Disagreements and arguments
- Difficulty performing work
- Carelessness
- Absenteeism and tardiness
- Secretive behavior
- Lying
- Indecisiveness
- Procrastination
- Self criticism/self blame
- Inertia
- Blaming others

II. Attitudinal indicators

- Unhappiness
- Frustration
- Irritability and agitation
- Hostility
- Hopelessness
- Despair
- Pessimism
- Preoccupation with problems
- Feeling overwhelmed
- Helplessness
- Guilt
- Lethargy
- Apathy
- Worrying
- Rigid, inflexible behavior
- Denial

III. Physical indicators

- Headaches
- Nausea
- Clumsiness
- Dizziness
- Fatigue

IV. Possible diagnoses

- Anxiety
- Depression
- Dependence or addiction
- Other:
  —Major physical illness
  —Major mental illness
  —Major life change

cal clues to detect the onset of problems then move swiftly to a preliminary diagnosis. The remarkable speed with which they intervene in problem situations reveals a bias toward action. Michael Weintraub, senior vice president of MedStat, a corporation that assesses health risk factors for business and industry, told us why he moves so quickly when he detects an ailment: "The sooner the intervention, the less risk there is for the worker and team. Too often, leaders wait to intervene out of fear of intruding on someone's privacy. However, the moment a behavioral problem or bad attitude arises on the job, it's a work issue that warrants discussion. The cost associated with leadership failure to intervene in a timely way runs into the tens of billions of dollars in the U.S. and Canada in one year."

Timely action depends on knowing what to look for. Workleaders possess a commanding knowledge of the types of behaviors, attitudes, and physical changes outlined in the Healing Needs Analyzer and they can tell the difference between a slight, temporary malady and a major, life-threatening one. Amazingly, exemplary leaders tend to respond even more quickly than healthcare clinicians, who we expected would cope with problems most swiftly. John Wolfe, a prominent healthcare CEO, explains why: "Clinicians are typically dealing reactively to problems that have become rather serious. They're more comfortable with disease management than prevention. Thus, they tend *not* to see small but marked changes as significant. By contrast, exceptional leaders think and act proactively. They seem to know intuitively when a change, however small, is significant."

John's observation parallels some alarming U.S. and Canadian statistics that show healthcare workers such as nurses suffer higher than average levels of stress-related disorders such as depression and substance dependency and abuse problems. Our research also documented that while healthcare workleaders record comparatively low levels of absenteeism and health problems compared to leaders in other industry sectors—a remarkable achievement given the data on healthcare—average leaders in nursing and other clinical areas suffer more serious absenteeism, stress, and dependency problems among their team members than do leaders in other fields. The costs associated with these problems for both the individual and the organization call for assertive action by leaders.

➤ A Script for Diagnosing—Mary's Story

Mary, a group vice president for an accounting services firm, recently observed noticeable changes in the behavior of Thelma, one of her team members. A skillful accountant, Thelma always appeared to balance her work and home lives with ease, but it seemed to Mary that something had recently thrown her life out of kilter. For several days Thelma forgot elements in key reports or handled them carelessly. Then one day she arrived at work distraught and unable to disguise her distress any longer. When Jim, her officemate, reminded her of a special out-of-town field audit assignment the next week, Thelma's temper boiled over and she accused Jim of keeping secrets and failing to schedule work properly.

Observing this interaction, Mary allowed an hour to pass while emotions cooled down, then invited Thelma to join her for a cup of coffee in her office. There, sitting side by side in front of her desk, Mary initiated a Healing Needs Analysis.

Mary: Thank you for joining me, Thelma. I've wanted to have a chance to catch up on things and find out how your work is going. *(Mary offers Thelma the opportunity to take the initiative. Mary knows that ultimately Thelma herself must recognize any problem.)*

Thelma: Well, things are going okay, I guess.

Mary: Care to elaborate?

Thelma: Well, there's really not much more to say. I'm just plugging along like everybody. *(Thelma's apathy and unhappiness provide a framework for a focused comment and question.)*

Mary: Well, Thelma, I don't think of you as someone who just plugs along. Have you been feeling well?

Thelma: Well, to tell you the truth, I've been extremely tired lately.

The first step in a healing intervention involves recognizing the signs of trouble. Through careful observation and a compassionate opening, Mary quickly gathers sufficient information to confirm the need for a healing intervention. Thelma has demonstrated forgetfulness, carelessness, difficulty performing her work well and on time, and blames others—her officemate Jim. In conversation, she reveals an atypical apathy and unhappiness. While the specific reasons for her difficulty and a complete diagnosis will take more probing, Mary decides that a healing intervention is in order.

By identifying behavioral, attitudinal, and physical changes, a workleader can assess when an associate needs assistance even if the associate does not always recognize that need. In our study, workleaders strove to identify sources of personal problems and stress, recognizing that proactive assessment can do a lot to prevent a serious crisis and reduce suffering.

➤ Tool #2: The Healing Guide

Using the Healing Needs Analyzer, Mary noted sufficient changes to warrant continuing her conversations with

Thelma. To do so, she can use Tool #2: The Healing Guide, which provides a structure for identifying both problems and possible solutions in a healing process that helps to recenter an associate in need.

Workleaders often distribute a copy of the Healing Guide as the conversation unfolds. Because emotional distress may make it hard for people to focus clearly on their problems, the Healing Guide provides a handy reference to keep the conversation as objective as possible. It also helps leaders define their own role as healer. The legal and ethical realities of today's work environment require that leaders involve themselves in associates' problems with the utmost care, and the Healing Guide helps to set the appropriate parameters for discussion and identify if and when a problem requires outside assistance.

The Healing Guide follows a progression of activities that helps both parties tackle a problem in manageable stages. Step 1 involves recognition of the signs of distress. The discussion of these signs is an act of involvement that helps reduce feelings of avoidance and disconnection. Build a bridge of understanding by helping the associate recognize a problem and admit that it has been hampering achievement.

This leads directly to Step 2, a discussion of work and personal stresses, and to Step 3, an analysis of life situation changes, including work and personal roles, relationships, and plans. From there it becomes easy to take Step 4 and attempt to identify the problem. Here the 80/20 rule comes in handy: Seek to identify the 20 percent of the problems that usually cause 80 percent of the trouble. Step 5 involves the critically important issue of defining the problem's level of urgency and importance. After moving through the first five steps to define a problem, you can apply the *100-year rule*: Ask an associate whether the problem will matter in 100 years. This question helps to clarify the urgency and importance of the situation, leading to Step 6, brainstorming solutions.

Brainstorming generates ideas without prejudging their merit. It attempts to look at a problem without any precon-

TOOL #2: THE HEALING GUIDE

1. Recognize the signs.
   - ➤ Look for patterns that undermine achievement.
   - ➤ Catch problems early.
   - ➤ Adapt an attitude of empathy and involvement.

2. Identify the stressors.
   - ➤ Determine work stressors.
   - ➤ Determine personal stressors.

3. Identify changes in the life situation.
   - ➤ Determine work and personal role changes.
   - ➤ Determine relationship changes.
   - ➤ Determine changes in plans.

4. Identify the problem.
   - ➤ Apply the 80/20 rule.

5. Evaluate urgency and importance.
   - ➤ Evaluate 4 categories.
     - • Problem is urgent and important.
     - • Problem is urgent and not important.
     - • Problem is not urgent but important.
     - • Problem is not urgent and not important.
   - ➤ Apply the 100-year rule.

6. Brainstorm solutions.
   - ➤ Start with a specific goal.
   - ➤ Frame the solution positively.
   - ➤ Ask how to reduce outside control.
   - ➤ Ask how to reduce inside control.

7. Select a solution.
   - ➤ Do what can be done.
   - ➤ Clarify the role to be taken.
   - ➤ Value yourself.
   - ➤ Recognize the possibility of change.
   - ➤ Choose solutions within your control.

8. Take action.

9. Evaluate results.

ceptions in an effort to produce a broad array of possible solutions. At Step 7 the workleader helps associates choose the solutions that lie within their personal control and that concentrate on improving their own performance. The goal is pragmatic: Focus on the positive and improve self-confidence and self-control by doing what can be done.

Once a solution is selected, take action and then evaluate the results in Steps 8 and 9. Workleaders believe that the best healing comes from accomplishment, and they follow the old admonition that if you fall off a horse you should get right back on and try again. They use the healing process to help people get back on the bicycle of life and resume their journey toward achievement as quickly as possible.

➤ A Script for the Healing Guide

Let's see how this script works by resuming Mary's inter-action with Thelma as Mary continues a formal healing interview.

> *Mary:* Thelma, based on what I've observed and your comments, I want to talk about your situation more specifically, using a Healing Guide. I think it will help us sort things out. Shall we start by reviewing some of the signs of trouble or jump ahead and identify stressors? *(Mary takes charge of the process but assists Thelma in accepting responsibility by offering her an option as to where she thinks she might start. Notice that Mary does not ask Thelma a yes or no question but one requiring a choice, a tactic that encourages responsibility and involvement.)*
>
> *Thelma:* Well, I'm not sure. What do you mean by the signs?

Mary: I've noticed a pattern of small but significant changes in your behavior these past few weeks that suggests you're going through a difficult period. Here's a copy of the list I used to identify them. You'll recall that earlier you mentioned that you felt like you were just plugging away and feeling fatigued, don't you? *(Thelma has obviously chosen Step 1 and needs to own the reality of the situation, which Mary helps her to do by reviewing the Healing Needs Analyzer.)*

Thelma: Well, yes, but anyone can feel a little off.

Mary: You're right. But, let me ask you, have you noticed that your concentration has slipped, and that you've been unusually forgetful and irritable? With Jim, for example. These are small but significant changes, not the Thelma I'm accustomed to. Wouldn't you agree? *(Mary helps Thelma focus on the problem, using questions to initiate involvement rather than statements she might perceive as accusations.)*

Thelma: I didn't know it was so obvious.

Mary: Taken together, these symptoms suggest a pattern of distress that I think we should analyze before it gets worse. Can you see what I've been seeing? *(When Mary puts her observations on the table for analysis, Thelma must respond and thus begin the healing process. By asking her whether she "can see what I see," Mary encourages her to reconnect and take responsibility for her actions.)*

Thelma: Mary, I had no idea my problems were showing up at work. I've always tried hard to keep my personal business from affecting my work.

Mary: Thelma, any of us can go through a rough time, and when we do, our personal concerns become the concerns of everyone around us because they affect our ability to serve each other and our customers. I'm here to help people sort through difficult situations. Are you ready to go to the next step and talk about the stressors that might be causing your discomfort? *(As Thelma begins to face reality, Mary moves her forward by explaining the context for their discussion and Mary's own role and responsibility in addressing the situation.)*

Thelma: Yes.

Mary: Good. Let's move on to stressors, our next step. *(Mary formally recognizes each step of progress both to build confidence and to mark Thelma's movement from avoidance and distress to involvement and action.)* If you're comfortable, let's talk about them formally. Are there any changes in your life that could impact your work? *(Mary asks Thelma to note any change, positive or negative, recognizing that the cumulative impact of change can itself be a source of stress. Notice how she frames her question in terms of work. Though she feels concern for Thelma on a personal level, she is careful to stay within the ethical and legal bounds of their work relationship.)*

Thelma: Well, I haven't wanted to burden anyone, but my husband, Ken, has been laid off.

Mary: I'm sorry to hear that. Was it sudden or expected? *(Mary probes for more information at every stage, pushing Thelma to think and cope.)*

Thelma: No more than my Mom's stroke. At least Ken is available to go to the nursing home now, even if I can't. My travel schedule hasn't allowed me to be with her much.

Mary: Those are all major problems, Thelma. When did they start? *(As Mary continues to probe, she uncovers the fact that in addition to her personal stressors Thelma is worried about her job's travel demands.)* Don't all of these things place a big burden on your roles at home and here? *(Once Thelma connects her personal life to her work, Mary can probe further on the personal level.)*

Thelma: Mary, everything is turned on its head. Now I'm the principal breadwinner and Ken's holding down the fort at home and with Mom. Before, he did the traveling and I was able to maintain a stable environment for our kids. They're in seventh and fourth grade, and I'm not there for them enough.

Mary: I understand. I've been there myself. Let's talk a little about how these role changes are affecting your work. Can you see a connection between your recent behavior and your performance? *(Mary has succeeded in getting Thelma to acknowledge role and relationship changes and pushes forward to help her understand the link between these and the behavioral changes at work.)*

Thelma: Yes, Mary, I'm beginning to see what's happened.

Mary: Should we begin to address the problem directly? Now that we understand the changes that have occurred, let's ask ourselves the most important question: What is the main problem we need to address? *(By moving systematically through the steps of the process,*

	Mary has helped Thelma identify the various issues impacting her life. Now she can identify the central challenge and the key to restabilizing her life.)
Thelma:	Well, one problem is finding Ken a job.
Mary:	Is that the main problem?
Thelma:	No, the kids would see less of him then, so would Mom.
Mary:	Is that the main problem? What's most important thing you need to do to address the various changes in your life? Can you see one solution that will give you the best chance to control your problems? *(Mary moves Thelma forward, reviewing all the changes until Thelma chooses an objective.)*
Thelma:	Well, the thing that has the most stress now is my job—keeping my job is now the key to holding the rest together.
Mary:	Then let's assume that's the central problem. How urgent and important is it? *(Mary again moves Thelma forward, to Step 6, urging her to measure the seriousness of the problem and thus the need for her to focus on it.)*
Thelma:	Mary, it's both urgent and important. Oh, God, I've just hung myself, haven't I?
Mary:	No, you haven't hung yourself, Thelma. On the contrary, you have accepted the responsibility to face up to a difficult situation. And I will admire you for it. Let's move forward, okay? How can you improve your ability to do your job? Let's brainstorm some answers. *(Mary directly and unequivocally answers Thelma's anxious question, providing positive*

reinforcement of constructive behavior and pushing directly forward to Step 6 where they brainstorm possible solutions together and create a concrete plan of action.)

Thelma: Well, I need to negotiate a change in responsibilities with Ken, but he's so stressed.

Mary: Don't prejudge the situation Thelma, just keep going. What else can you do? Let's keep an objective in mind: how to help you keep and succeed in your job. *(Mary coaches Thelma on creatively exploring options without prejudice. Together they create a list that includes: reestablishing rapport with Jim, her officemate; speaking to the children about a change in work schedules and home roles; and setting up schedules for visits with her mother.)* We've got quite a list of possible solutions. Now we can apply some criteria to sort things out. Let's look at Step 7. Notice the very first item: Do what can be done. Is there anything on this list that can't be done? *(Mary applies each of the criteria to the proposed solutions, finding that all of them provide constructive options: They can be done; they help Thelma improve her sense of control.)* Of these solutions, which do you think is the key, the one that will help solve all the others?

Thelma: Perhaps taking the initiative rather than playing the victim with respect to all of the things that have happened in my life recently.

Mary: I couldn't agree with you more. And I want to assure you that I'll be here to help sort things out as we go along. I have one more suggestion to offer. Before your trip next week, why don't you take a day or two off now to implement your plans? Then, after your trip, let's get together to see how it's working. *(Mary moves the meeting to closure by offering support that allows for immediate action, evaluation, and follow-up.)*

In this scenario, Mary intervenes in a direct and effective way by following a systematic prescription of self-healing. Psychologists call this process *cognitive therapy,* the analysis of the interactions between feelings and behavior. By studying the patterns of cause and effect, anyone can think his or her way out of crisis and devise a strategy to reassert self-control. Workleaders demonstrate a classic cognitive therapeutic approach as they apply the Healing Guide within professional parameters.

Throughout the process, workleaders bear in mind their foremost responsibility: to serve the customer. In this context, they assert themselves whenever they think changes in personal, team, or organizational behavior can negatively affect service. This contrasts with a more formal therapeutic role where the therapist might hold back until the patient requests assistance.

Workleaders recognize that they are not therapists and should not function in that capacity. Their interactions must remain within the bounds of the work relationship. Mary helped Thelma focus on how they could work together to protect Thelma's fine record of achievement and thus the job that meant so much to Thelma's family security. By doing so, Mary displayed not only compassion for Thelma but also unreserved commitment to the customer.

Like all workleaders, Mary also maintained her role focus and thereby helped Thelma to reestablish her own role. Had Mary moved from her professional role as workleader to that of a personal friend or therapist, she would have undermined the already fragile platform on which Thelma found herself. Finally, Mary used the nine-step Healing Guide both to manage the process and to evaluate the severity of Thelma's problem. If Thelma had not been able to move through the process efficiently, Mary would have known to call for outside help. If significant progress is not made in two counseling sessions, outside help may be the answer.

➤ Healing a Whole Organization—Chuck's Story

Charles Thomas built a career of achievement as a social worker, advocate for the poor, and administrator of state and federal agencies. Throughout those 35 years he had mastered the role of the healer, but he found that mastery taxed to the limit when he agreed to take on a mission impossible— cleaning up the social services mess in Oslo County. He accepted the assignment because he knew that the suffering caused by decades of bad policy and lack of commitment affected not only the system's customers—the indigent and abandoned and abused children—but the deliverers of service as well. The governor and the state commissioner hired Chuck with the mandate to make "whatever changes are necessary," even if it meant "blowing it up."

Chuck knew that a tough-guy approach was not the answer, however. Sure, he would have to throw out some bad apples, but as he had learned over the years, real healing must address the wounds of the survivors. How could anyone expect the social services staff to demonstrate empathy and exercise discipline if the leader himself did not bring these behaviors to bear on the situation?

After three weeks on the job meeting with department heads, clients, citizens' groups, and city and county officials, an event occurred that unexpectedly revealed the right prescription for the ailing system. It happened after several days of long and tedious meetings with staff about the need for greater sensitivity to client needs.

Gloria Frazier, head of Children's Services, burst into Chuck's office with news that a new security guard had harassed a young mother whose abusive husband insisted that she was unfit to have custody of her child. She arrived at the custody hearing distraught over being separated from her son and strip searched for weapons, and had done little to represent her position well, which may, in fact, have cost her custody of the boy. When Gloria said, "These damn guards have got to be put in their place," Chuck decided only he could do it. "Let's send a message everyone will hear," he concluded. Then he called the guard, Norm Peyton, and his supervisor into his office.

Chuck: Norm, I understand you were on duty this morning when Mrs. Holden and her son arrived for custody hearings. Is that right?

Norm: Well, I don't really know. I'm new here. There were so many people. I, uh, I . . .

Chuck: Well, I understand that the mother was strip searched and, in effect, emotionally harassed. Did you know that she was heading for a custody hearing and that she arrived here so upset that she made a terrible impression on her case worker—a fact that may have cost her custody of her little boy?

Norm: No. My God. I never intended to do any harm. You know, I was told to apply the new security regulations by the book. I'm really sorry. What can I do?

Chuck: Well, nothing now. We're tending to it. Let's let things cools down, and we'll talk tomorrow.

However, when Chuck called the next morning to talk with Norm, the guard had not reported to work. In fact, he didn't show up all that day or the next. Chuck explains what happened: "As soon as Norm left our meeting I knew I had done harm. I had jumped to conclusions and failed to analyze needs, stressors, and changes—all the things I had talked to the staff about. I hoped Norm would show up the next day so I could finesse things and get back on track. But he didn't."

Chuck faced an ironic and humbling predicament. Mandated to heal the staff, he had instead injured someone. Instead of restoring calm, he found himself caught up in the "stress and mess," as the staff referred to it. And sent to clean house and bring in new blood, he had instead apparently killed off a newcomer who naively blundered on his first day.

Chuck faced an extraordinary healing challenge, but not the one he had anticipated. He had been searching for a pivotal event to turn things around, but didn't expect it to come as a result of his own poor performance. Nevertheless, when it arrived he responded. When Norm failed to show up the morning of the second day, Chuck did what an exceptional leader should do: Through a profound act of strategic humility, he accepted the responsibility to heal. "I had wronged Norm, but more important, I'd also demonstrated just the type of behavior I was determined to correct. The only thing to do was to face up to it. So, I called Norm up and apologized. I asked him if he would meet me for a cup of coffee. I remember the conversation as if it was yesterday."

Chuck: Norm, thank you for meeting with me. I wouldn't blame you if you didn't. But it's obvious that you're deeply concerned about our clients, too, and I respect your commitment. I want to apologize for my behavior and my failure to ask for your help rather than jump to conclusions. I can only say that my behavior shows the influence of the stressors that everyone is facing at the agency. I hope you'll accept my apology. *(Through his apology, Chuck uses himself to teach the need for analysis and the healing process. He reaches out to Norm by giving him the chance to assert control through accepting the apology. This is a critical step to rebuilding the control and self-esteem that Norm lost due to the incident.)*

Norm: Of course I accept, Chuck. I could see that everyone is stressed and uptight. It's easy to lose it.

Chuck: Yes, it is. I understand that much better now. Do you think that others see the signs of distress and understand what's causing the problems? *(Chuck begins to move Norm along the healing path, offering him the option of Step 1, recognizing the signs of stress, or Step 2, identifying stressors.)*

Norm: Man, I don't know. They seem so uptight I don't think they can see it. I'm new and it's really obvious to me.

Chuck: That's a very interesting insight. One of the reasons I took this job was because I believed I could bring a fresh perspective but, well, I haven't been following my own advice. Norm, we're trying to help a lot of people who need help and save the public money to boot. We're going to launch a series of meetings with the staff to rebuild confidence and client focus. It means working carefully through a ten-step process where we put our cards on the table to recognize the signs of distress, identify the causes of stress and hurt—like my off-the-wall remarks—and identify problems and their solutions—and most importantly, to put those solutions into action. We need team leaders to help with this and I think you're just the kind of person to help. Would you consider helping us heal our wounds and move forward?

Norm: Well, I need to think about it a little, but it does sound like something that's really needed.

Chuck: It really is. I can attest to it personally. Listen, just let me know tomorrow when you come back. Or do you think you can come back today? I want you to know that I have publicly told the team that I was going to personally apologize to you for my behavior. I need you, and everyone else wants me to tell you, they need you back too. *(Chuck gives Norm options but not yes or no, thus making him more likely to choose to reconnect.)*

As it turned out, Norm came back that afternoon and subsequently participated as a team leader in guiding the agency through the ten-step healing process, using the Healing Needs Analyzer to prime the pump and the Healing Guide to take them through an orderly and therapeutic process of renewal.

■ FULFILLING THE ROLE OF THE HEALER

Chuck's story illustrates one of the most simple but powerful dimensions of healing: The courage to admit one's human frailty and to recognize the potential for renewal and healing that each of us possesses.

We began this chapter with a discussion of Lincoln as a healer. His humanity and humility were driven by visionary genius and unwavering discipline. Healing is not for the faint of heart. It takes resolve, tenacity, and an ability to focus thinking in the midst of intense emotional and physical injury. Mary and Chuck exhibit similar qualities and provide us with practical insight into application of the healing process in our contemporary work lives, whether in one-on-one or team situations. This type of resolve is also demonstrated in the role of the protector, the subject of our next chapter.

8

The Protector

During the Great Depression in the 1930s, President Roosevelt's Interior Secretary once complained, "I wish that Mrs. Roosevelt would stick to her knitting and keep out of the affairs connected with my department." Like many at the time, he found Eleanor Roosevelt's actions too radical to be popular. But as she and FDR knew, radical action was called for to protect the welfare of the nation.

Before FDR took office in 1933, First Ladies were carefully guarded from the press and public. But only six days after her husband's inauguration Eleanor Roosevelt set about revolutionizing the position of First Lady by holding the first of her regular press conferences to explain her role as FDR's eyes and ears. She had played that part before. During FDR's comeback from polio, Eleanor herself traveled the political hustings to learn about people's needs and to gain support for FDR. Together they built the most remarkable husband and wife team in the history of American leadership. As the Depression ground on and the nation's thoughts turned towards war, Eleanor devoted more and more of her time to the cause of protecting core individual values. Searching the fault lines of American culture for signs of conflict, turmoil, and distress, she worked tirelessly as an advocate, problem solver, and fighter as needed.

Concerned about the Depression's effects on the nation's children, Eleanor fought to create the National Youth Administration (NYA), which FDR signed into law in 1935. Though many Americans objected to the legislation because NYA programs were open to blacks and whites alike, Eleanor battled such divisive segregationist views because of the deep threat they held for a society already divided by poverty. In 1939 at a Southern Conference for Human Welfare in Alabama she reminded everyone that a house divided will surely fall. When Eleanor sat to listen to other speakers at the conference she disobeyed a segregation law and sat with the black participants. When the conference authorities approached her to object, she moved her chair to the middle of the aisle, squarely between the black and the white audience members.

Eleanor recognized that as the United States plunged headlong into World War II, democratic liberty would become its defining national ethic. She and FDR had agreed that together they must confront each and every threat to the nation's core ethical ideals. Otherwise the nation could easily languish in moral and political uncertainty. Thus, when the Daughters of the American Revolution (DAR) refused to let the renowned African-American contralto Marian Anderson perform in their Constitution Hall, the only venue large enough to accommodate Anderson's fans, Eleanor intervened. While the First Lady had always considered herself a proud member of the DAR, she immediately resigned her membership in protest. Her actions focused worldwide attention on the issue and people across the nation hailed her defense of principles the country had fought for less than eighty years earlier. The Roosevelt Department of the Interior then sponsored a free open-air concert on the steps of the Lincoln Memorial. More than 75,000 people gathered to hear Marian Anderson sing.

Recognizing her unique contributions to the protection of the ideals of universal kinship, President Truman appointed Eleanor to lead the U.S. delegation at the first meeting of the United Nations Assembly in 1948. She chaired the United Nations' Human Rights Division and spearheaded the development of the Declaration of Human Rights. Upon its passage the entire assembly gave her a standing ovation. That honor remains a unique recognition in the annals of world leadership. Eleanor Roosevelt's skill as a protector transcended the boundaries of nation, race, and religion to address threats to the well-being of people everywhere. She understood both the ideological and practical need to stand firm in the face of adversity and to take personal responsibility to protect.

■ THE ROLE OF THE PROTECTOR

The protector responds to crises that threaten to tear people and organizations apart. Like Eleanor Roosevelt, the workleaders in our study proved themselves expert risk managers. They believe that while terrible events can ambush them and their people at any time, they can always deal with the most difficult circumstances and even turn them into opportunities. As learned optimists, they meet challenges head-on and overcome them with patience and perseverance. Inner toughness and resilience provide the best protection for them, the customer, and those who serve the customer. Patience, perseverance, and hardiness allow them to identify and prepare for any eventuality ahead of time. Everyday workleaders maintain a *crisis approach* mentality that prepares them to approach the possibility of crisis as an opportunity for growth.

Their crisis approach mentality prompts them to develop a set of skills for managing the core condition of any crisis: conflict. Regardless of the nature of a risk—technical, economic, social, operational, or natural—the threat of conflict accompanies it. Such conflict can take the form of unproductive territorial squabbles, finger-pointing, or anxiety-driven runs for cover that divert human energy from addressing the substantive issues behind the risks. Workleaders develop a concrete protocol to separate ego from issue and sort through the emotional inflammation surrounding a risk in order to identify the opportunities to overcome and move beyond it.

In the same way that Eleanor Roosevelt searched the front lines of American society for threats during the Depression, workleaders have learned to spot signs of impending crisis and conflict. When those signs appear they are ready to respond rapidly. Whether workleaders have explicitly prepared themselves for a particular risk or not, their preparation provides a methodology for action in any situation. George Armitage, a retired colonel in the U.S. Air Force and managing partner of an international financial crisis management consulting firm, explained the importance of such preparation: "The key to risk management is understanding the universal process by which a risk turns into a threat. Invariably, it hits like a bombshell, spreading confusion and fear. At its core, however, every threat has a simple reality. By mastering the skills that cut through the chaos to the core problem, you can be prepared to reduce a threat from a crisis level to problem-solving level in short order. The threat itself is never exactly as you planned, but the process needed to manage it is."

Because workleaders strive so diligently to protect their core values and those of the people they serve, they experience 20 to 40 percent lower levels of conflict and crisis than average leaders, as measured by such indicators as labor grievances and work actions, customer service and quality problems, financial losses or budget overruns, unplanned employee turnover, and legal problems such as malpractice suits. When conflicts and crises do erupt, workleaders in all fields universally win praise from others in their organizations as the most effective individuals to deal with such situations. They address crises in less than half the time of average leaders, either by resolving the conflict or implementing an effective plan of corrective action.

In order to clarify our workleaders' approach to crisis management, we have organized the skills of the protector into two tools, the *Risk Assessment Guide* and the *Conflict Management Guide*. Together these tools provide a system for protecting an organization and its stakeholders against any and all threats to their mission and survival. The following chart provides an overview of these tools.

ROLE OF THE PROTECTOR

Goal: Diagnose and respond to threats to organizational well-being.

Method: Risk assessment and conflict management
➤ Anticipate the risk.
➤ Assess the risk with Tool #1: The Risk Assessment Guide.
  • Identify the type of risk.
  • Whom or what does the risk affect?
  • Identify the level of risk.
  • Identify the risk's likely duration.
➤ Plan to take charge.
➤ Learn from the risk.
➤ Manage conflict with Tool #2: The Conflict Management Guide.
  • Follow the principles of action.
  • Apply the ten-step plan of action.

Workleaders shun the conventional definition of *crisis* as an aberrant event in an otherwise orderly world, viewing it instead as a normal occurrence in a disorderly world. Their basic attitude about life is a variation of the old Murphy's Law that whatever can go wrong will go wrong. They know crisis will come, but they have prepared themselves to assess risk quickly and manage conflict skillfully. They recognize that what threatens their organizational well-being also often opens the door to greater achievement.

➤ Tool #1: The Risk Assessment Guide

While workleaders use the Risk Assessment and Conflict Management Guides concurrently in real protection situations, we will examine each separately before combining them in a case study later in the chapter. The Risk Assessment Guide includes three distinct stages:

THE RISK ASSESSMENT GUIDE

Stage I: Anticipate the risk.

➤ Identify the type of risk.
- Strategic
- Sales
- Operational
- Technical
- Ethical
- Legal
- Political
- Cultural
- Personal
- Economic

➤ Where is the risk coming from?
- Individual
- Group
- Organization
- Natural force or event

➤ What is the level of risk: High ⇔ Low?

➤ What is the likely duration: Short ⇒ Long-term?

Stage II: Plan to take charge.

➤ Establish an objective.
➤ Consult those you lead.
➤ Act boldly.
➤ Dominate the situation.
➤ Lead by example.

Stage III: Learn from the risk.

➤ What were the consequences?
➤ Did we respond well?
➤ What is the risk now? (Repeat Stage I.)

The Risk Assessment Guide follows a three-stage process: Assessment and analysis serve as bookends to planning and action. Since people cannot act if they do not understand, workleaders emphasize assessment throughout the crisis management process.

During Stage I, workleaders anticipate risk. As seasoned veterans of life's surprises they understand that the risk of crisis always exists. They routinely view events in terms of risk type and source and produce a practical taxonomy to help them understand a situation. They also assess a risk's level and expected duration, which enables them to estimate the overall impact of any event should it escalate into an active threat or overt crisis. Paradoxically, workleaders combine belief in the old Murphy's Law with belief in a new Murphy's Law: "Anything that should go right, can go right." Jack Burke, owner of a rapidly expanding computer skills training center, resolves the apparent contradiction: "When you look the sources of fear in the eye, you become liberated. By recognizing that life has risk you pass from doubt to certainty, and from *wondering* whether you should charge ahead with living to *knowing* with certainty that you should and can—there is only one viable course of action and that is to take control."

As Jack points out, risk assessment leads inexorably to the desire to take charge. Here workleaders retain strict discipline and plan their moves deliberately even in urgent situations. Average leaders, on the other hand, tend to rush headlong into action at this point, but Dr. James Pepicello, surgeon and COO of Hamot Health Foundation in Erie, Pennsylvania, tells us why they shouldn't: "The greatest leaders are diagnosticians and planners, who think up to and through their actions. When a surgical case starts, I continue to stay in a diagnostic and planning mode, looking for what's best for my patient. When a critically ill patient arrives in the emergency department, the physician continues to plan even while diagnosing and taking action. You never just rush headlong into action; that's how you lose control."

Continuous review (Stage III) provides the capacity to learn from the risk. Here conduct a formal review. In Dr. Pepicello's words, "In medicine, we are compelled to evaluate risk on both ends of and during an intervention. It's called the *clinical model* and becomes a conditioned response that, I think, provides a wonderful model for leadership risk management in any setting. As a COO, I use it routinely."

Let's see how anyone can translate Dr. Pepicello's clinical model of assessment, intervention, and evaluation into action when faced with a business threat.

➤ A Script for Assessing Risk

Tony Erardi, the general manager for Kellman Foods, a regional New England food distribution company specializing in seafood, has grown concerned about newspaper reports recording declining tonnage for catches off the Georges Bank, the principal source of his company's fresh cod, halibut, and other kinds of fish. This information coincides with similar reports regarding the lobster catches from Boston up the Maine coast. Tony has convened a risk assessment meeting for his senior management team: Jack Winston, Warehouse Manager; Rob Gruber, Sales Manager; and Gwen Kin, Business Office Manager. They follow the Risk Assessment Guide to focus their conversation.

> *Tony:* Thanks for coming. I think you've all had a chance to review the fish and lobster production reports. I expect to hear from our suppliers within the week that they're true and that we can expect lower-volume shipments. I'd like us to think through the implications of this using a Risk Assessment Guide. Let's take the first step and anticipate the type of risk this situation presents. *(Tony guides attention to the specific threat.)*

Rob: Aggravated customers—dropping sales, that's the first risk. And that's strategic. We've built this business as a specialty house. If we can't get the fish, we're marginalized out of the market.

Gwen: Rob, just charge more. If we can't, we'll end up with a huge loss. And Tony, just figure that if fish sales go down ten percent, we have to decrease overhead seven to eight percent. Assume ten percent loss of fish, and we're twenty to twenty-five percent the size we are now.

Tony: Bad news, huh. I'm glad you're not holding back, but let's take things a step at a time. Rob and Gwen, the two of you have identified strategic sales and marketing and economic risks right off the top. Give me a sense of the risk level, just for the books, though I know by the tone of your voices what it is. *(Tony uses the Guide to keep Rob and Gwen from moving too far too fast.)*

Rob: From a sales and strategic point of view, I'd say it's high risk and, though you didn't ask, I'll bet it could be long-term.

Gwen: High, high, high, and God knows how long. The bottom line is this: Jack should start planning layoffs now, and we should cancel the capital purchases we've got in the pipeline.

Tony: Good point, Gwen, but we're going too fast. We'll get a plan of action soon. Jack, what's your call?

Jack: We face a series of risks. Our warehouse operations will need to be streamlined. Legally, the union is going to go through the roof and could try to close us down altogether. And personally, well, let's say I don't want to go out in the warehouse right now without a Kevlar jacket.

Tony: I understand—I worked there for years. Well, I'm glad you folks aren't shy about sharing your feelings. But, you know, there's one thing we didn't identify. Where's the risk coming from?

Gwen: Well, looking at your Guide, it's obviously a force of nature. I mean, no individual, group, or organization is purposely not catching or selling us fish.

Tony: Right. And I think that offers us a possible launching point for taking charge of this situation. This is a no-fault threat. It gives us an objective platform for launching a far-reaching, open discussion of what we need to do. All of us—customers, management, ownership, employees, the union—are in it together. That's what we've got to emphasize. *(Tony moves to the second stage of the assessment.)*

    Let me tell you what I mean. First of all, I'm going to clarify the nature of the risk, whether it's as high as we fear it is. The catches are down, but not so far that we won't get any fish. They're probably down ten to twenty percent in volume. We need a specific plan to address each of the risks you identified. Our objective will be to meet problems arising from a ten percent to twenty percent shortfall of fish. I want each of you to consult with your staff about what you need to do. Then I want your best and most creative ideas. Come back tomorrow at 3:00 with five to ten ideas each. We will then work out a plan and have it ready by tomorrow night. Can you change your plans if you need to stay through dinner? If and when this threat hits, we are going to be ready and take charge. And I want our people to know we're on top of it and involved. *(Tony explains how the process works, teaching and leading by example, providing a role model for what needs to be done and how to take charge through assessment.)*

Jack: Tony, are you sure you want me to consult with my folks? That means the union, too, you know.

Tony: Tell you what, Jack. I'll talk to the local union president myself. I'll call him right after this meeting. I do want you to talk with your supervisors and office staff to get operational input. Present it as a possible concern based on reports in the press. Let's keep calm, but let's begin preparing our people. They've already read the reports. I know that because Harry, one of the truck drivers, told me. They'll get more jittery if we don't appear to be on top of things.

Gwen: Tony, if we're lucky enough to get through this time, there's likely to be a next time.

Tony: Gwen, I understand your concern and I agree. Let me to say two things. First, we will get through this—not by luck, but by assessment and planning. Second, as we go through this, we'll be thinking about what it can teach us. We're going to stick with this and plan how to minimize the risk for the future. *(Tony reinforces the process and the need to follow through.)*

Rob: I can tell you one thing—we've got to be more than a one-product company.

Tony: That's exactly the kind of thinking we need, Rob. Keep track of what you're learning. But, there's one caution. Right now, at this moment, we *are* a one-product operation. So let's be sure not to blame our strategic misfortune. Let's meet this challenge first. Okay? *(Tony reinforces the need to retain discipline of the process and focus on planning, not blaming.)*

All: Okay.

Tony: Then I'll see you all at 3 P.M. tomorrow. If any-
           one needs to talk, see me anytime.

Tony has used the Risk Assessment Guide to launch his
team in the right direction, preparing them to confront the
threat through analysis, planning, and evaluation rather
than fear and blame. Now they stand poised to take charge
and act boldly and decisively. Throughout the process, however, Tony has emphasized that thinking, not emotions, will
rule their actions, that they will confront threats as a team,
and that they will turn fear and negativity into resolve and
optimism.

➤ Tool #2: The Conflict Management Guide

The possibility of interpersonal conflict always attends crisis. Tony's fish supply crisis, driven by national fishing fleets
overfishing already depleted waters, has ignited intense feelings among the fleets and has set the stage for potentially
violent conflict between nations. When conflict or crises
visit the lives of groups or individuals, the resulting tension,
stress, and frustration can lead to turmoil. Often, however,
the conflict itself is the first symptom of risk. Workleaders
have developed a protocol for translating such situations into
opportunities for risk prevention and problem solving.

As workleaders explained their strategy for conflict management to us, it became evident that nine basic principles
guide their actions. The first of these derives from workleaders' ever-present optimism and their understanding that the
confusion and frustration of conflict offer an opportunity
for taking initiative and demonstrating personal resolve.
These efforts should focus immediately on finding ways to
contain the conflict. Like a virus, an outbreak of crisis can
spread confusion and frustration with lightning speed.

TOOL #2: THE CONFLICT MANAGEMENT GUIDE

A. Learn principles of action.

1. Use confusion and conflict as opportunities to take the initiative.
2. Assess the risk personally.
3. Contain the risk and minimize contamination.
4. Never align yourself with criticism of others without validating the matter yourself.
5. Correct misrepresentations or false charges immediately.
6. Address one conflict or risk at a time.
7. Minimize formal conflict through persuasion and dialogue.
8. Make conflicting parties responsible for their own behavior by guiding their dialogue.
9. Constantly measure solutions against the values and mission of the organization.

B. Apply the plan of action.

Step 1. Listen to Party A.
Step 2. Observe.
Step 3. Listen to Party A.
Step 4. Problem solve with Party B.
Step 5. Meet with Parties A and B.
Step 6. Clarify each party's position.
Step 7. Guide dialogue.
Step 8. Search for a solution.
Step 9. Seek consensus.
Step 10. Implement a decision.

Conflict is so potentially explosive that leaders should never align themselves with a criticism that could feed conflict without first personally validating the matter. This becomes especially important if views have been misrepresented or false charges have been leveled. Conflict is fraught with emotion, and false accusations or slander can simply pour gasoline on the fire. Because conflict can explode, leaders should focus their complete energies on extinguishing it and never divide their resources by trying to douse the fires of conflict on more than one front at a time.

A conflict's explosive potential is a direct function of the energy committed to it by conflicting parties. Intervention should therefore aim to transform that energy into productive channels—begin by helping the conflicting parties accept responsibility for their actions. To this end, a leader must assess the threat the conflict poses to the organization's values and mission and then guide a dialogue grounded in this assessment. One essential rule applies: The leader intervenes on behalf of the customers and those who serve them.

To translate the nine principles of the Conflict Management Guide into action, workleaders employ a ten-step conflict management script shaped by pragmatism and mission focus. The signs of conflict typically emerge during routine conversations with associates. At Step 1 for example, during a conversation with Party A regarding work, the symptoms of conflict may appear when Party A makes a critical remark or—if the situation has already become intense—an accusation against Party B. People often make such accusations in the heat of the moment as a displacement mechanism for aggressive feelings that arise due to work frustration. Recognizing this possibility, workleaders simply listen and respond with a noncommittal "I understand your concern" comment, but take no overt action at that moment to intervene. Instead they observe and monitor the situation (Step 2).

Knowing that they can actually create or spread conflict by overreacting publicly, workleaders react to complaints neutrally and privately. Doing so is consistent with the principles of behavioral psychology, which confirm that positive support of any kind can reinforce behavior. Therefore they proceed with all due restraint and discipline, regardless of the intensity of emotion the parties to the conflict are displaying.

A key signal of a conflict's contaminating potential arises if Party A complains again (Step 3). When this occurs a workleader knows the time has arrived to initiate action with Party B (Step 4), but—mindful of the need to minimize contamination—the workleader approaches Party B in a nonthreatening problem-solving consultation. Recognizing that Party B may see the situation entirely differently or not even be aware of any conflict with Party A, the workleader simply asks Party B to review To Do(s) and roadblocks: "What must you accomplish, and what's getting in the way of doing it?"

As we discussed in Chapter 4, a leader can insert the problem-solving interview into virtually any situation to focus people on the core issue of service. Through this approach, the workleader can gain insight into both Party B's awareness of the conflict and its potential consequences for customer service. Armed with this information, the workleader can then call both parties together for a dialogue (Step 5).

This conflict management strategy differs somewhat from some conventional teachings that advocate bringing individuals together immediately to explore possible conflicts. When we asked workleaders why they didn't bring people together right away, they reacted much like Carol Satterlee, a store manager for Wal-Mart, who reminded us that "The key issue here is protecting the customer, not my professional reputation or popularity with employees. Calling a meeting first thing is almost a knee-jerk reaction in management and it's almost always wrong, not right. At the beginning stages of a conflict, I need to collect information and consult one on one. When I've got a handle on things and understand the likely implications of the conflict for our customers and the rest of the team, then I'm ready to meet."

Workleaders take control of any meeting between two or more parties by calling everyone's attention to a difference of opinion or open conflict that could impair the organization's ability to provide quality customer service. The workleader then proceeds to ask each party to confirm and/or clarify present awareness and understanding of the conflict (Step 6). This encourages each party to accept responsibility for his or her own behavior and drives home an extraordinarily important principle: Conflicts and problems should be discussed in terms of the organization's mission, not in terms of personal interests.

Often, an individual associate or group will seek to manipulate a leader by asking him or her to maintain inappropriate confidentiality. Workleaders know that these requests are often manipulative. After each party presents a view on the situation, workleaders guide the dialogue by asking them to acknowledge that there are significant differences (Step 7) and that these differences could impact the team's ability to provide service to both customers and each other.

The act of openly acknowledging the conflict and its potential to inflict harm reinforces a sense of personal responsibility and the workleader's authority to move the dialogue forward with both problem-solving and negotiating scripts that identify possible solutions (Step 8) and reach consensus (Step 9). If consensus proves elusive, workleaders adjourn the meeting to explore options more fully in preparation for another attempt during a second meeting. But first they reinforce the need to find a solution that protects the organization's mission and formally reminds everyone that they must finally agree on implementing a decision. While exemplary leaders always strive toward consensus, they never hesitate to step in and make a decision required to protect the customer (Step 10). In very few cases during our study did workleaders overtly assert their legitimate authority as the boss, but they did so fairly often when managing conflict, laying down the law when absolutely necessary. Even as they did so, however, they kept in mind the consequences of their actions and the need to provide both an orderly process for implementing decisions and a mission-grounded context for their actions.

Let's now listen in as Patrick William, a foreman of an international firm called Global Contractors, which specializes in masonry construction, deals with a conflict.

➤ A Script for Managing Conflict

Pat routinely works with multinational work teams in South America, Asia, and the Middle East who literally don't speak the same language. Over the years he has learned the importance of assessing and, if necessary, responding rapidly to situations that could explode into physical conflict. As a result he's become a master protector. We listen in as he addresses such a challenge on a bridge construction project in Mexico City.

Pat approaches Dave, the site foreman.

Pat: Good morning, Dave. Is your crew ready to pour the pier footing this morning? *(Pat initiates contact at Step 1. The pier he refers to supports the bridge platform over the San Miguel river in the northeastern part of the city.)*

Dave: No, Pat, we're not ready, as usual. And, you can blame José's form construction team. They were supposed to have it done yesterday, but they goofed off. We work like dogs and they stand around waiting for an engraved invitation.

Pat: I understand you're angry, Dave, but let's just focus on the pier for the moment. Will you be able to pour in an hour?

Dave: Yes. But I want you to know we are going to fall behind schedule if those guys don't get moving.

Pat: I hear you, Dave, but let's just focus on the pier right now. Okay? *(Pat acknowledges Dave's concern but focuses the conversation on the work at hand for two reasons. First, he wants to focus energy on meeting customer goals. And second, he wants to assess the situation himself. He observes Dave's preparations—Step 2—while he carries out some administrative duties. He approaches Dave again—Step 3—an hour later.)*

Pat: Dave, are you pouring the pier yet?

Dave: Just starting. We'll make it, Pat. Today, that is. I tell you, José is a screw-up and you'd better do something.

Pat: I hear you.

Dave: That's what you said before. Are you going to do something or not?

Pat: Dave, I did hear you and I understand you're angry at José. Your job is to pour concrete and tell me about any problems you might have. You did that. Now it's my problem. Let me handle my job and you do yours, okay? You concentrate on pouring the pier; I don't want anybody getting hurt. All right? *(Pat forcefully defines his job responsibilities and establishes his own authority to deal with José. At the same time he focuses Dave on the task at hand.)*

Dave: Yeah, all right. *(Pat sees that the conflict has not extinguished itself and knows he must get to the bottom of it quickly. He also realizes he must approach José—Step 4—who has been under a lot of pressure to maintain a schedule himself.)*

Pat: José, got a minute?

José: Oh, hi, Pat. Yeah, but only a minute. We're busy as hell.

Pat: Tell me about it. What's your team doing today and is there anything that could get in the way of getting it done? *(Pat uses the problem-solving script to approach José, asking about To Do(s) and roadblocks. He does not mention the conflict yet since he wants to assess José's situation objectively. Raising it as an entry question would contaminate the situation with emotion and raise questions about his own integrity.)*

José: Well, we've got some form reconstruction problems. Dave's crew has been having trouble transporting the concrete to the pier site so they've jerry-built a bridge across the forms we constructed. I understand his problem, but it's knocking the hell out of the forms. So we have to go back and repair them, which slows us up.

Pat: I see. Did you know that Dave's concerned about the delays? *(Pat touches on the conflict.)*

José: *He's* concerned? I'm the one taking the hit.

Pat: Well, there's got to be a simple solution to the problem. Tell you what, meet me at the trailer for lunch. We'll get Dave there, too. *(Pat calls a meeting with both parties—Step 5—at the trailer that serves as a field office, where he can clarify each party's situation—Step 6. All three convene for lunch.)*

Pat: José, Dave, thanks for coming. I know both of you are under the gun and that we've got some problems to solve if we're going to meet the schedule. Let me see if I've got the situation straight. Dave, you're worried that José's team is going to slow you down by not having the forms ready for pouring, right? *(Pat immediately takes control of the meeting and sets a positive, problem-solving tone. He separates ego from issue by zeroing in on the practical work problems Dave faces rather than commenting on and thereby reinforcing his anger. He also lets both men know that work, not politics and self-interest, comes first.)*

Dave: Well, slowing me down is a little strong. I'm just concerned about getting my job done.

Pat: Dave, let me get this straight. You were late pouring the pier this morning because the forms weren't ready. Right?

Dave: Yeah.

Pat: And you told me you thought José's team was falling behind. Right?

Dave: Well, sort of.

Pat: Look, Dave, it's not sort of. I have a concern here. I need to understand your point of view clearly if I'm going to help. So, tell us, what is it? *(Pat refuses to be manipulated. He states the problem in nonaccusatory terms—"I have a concern"—and explains why clarification is necessary: "if I'm going to help." He clearly puts responsibility on Dave's shoulders, where it belongs.)*

Dave: Well, what I meant was that José has a heck of a challenge getting the forms constructed, and it worries me that his delay becomes my delay.

Pat: And that's it, Dave? Nothing else? *(Pat gives Dave the chance to share his point of view completely before asking José's opinion. Typically, the order of questioning follows the order in which the issue arose. Dave raised it first.)* José, how do you see things?

José: Well, sure we're late. But that's because Dave's crew is beating up our forms by using them as a bridge to get to the pier. We spend half our time reconstructing our original work.

Pat: How about that, Dave? Were you aware of José's problem? *(Pat moves back and forth to seek clarification, always involving the parties in facing up to their responsibilities for owning the situation. This sets the stage for finding a solution at Step 7.)*

Dave: Oh, I hadn't thought of that. I've been up to here in my own problems. Well, hell, I'm sorry, José, but I didn't know how else to transport the cement without laying planks over your forms.

José: Well, I know; that's why we didn't complain and just tried to fix them as fast as we could. *(Pat lets the dialogue flow naturally and then steps in to move it to the next step.)*

Pat: Both of you guys are working as hard as you can, and I want you both to know I appreciate it. I should have seen this coming, too, and now that we all understand the problem, let's find a solution. What about that new scaffolding technique we saw last week? *(Pat has averted a serious conflict, but he knows that loss of face for Dave could lead to more anger unless he can help both parties focus on implementing a solution that gives both reason to feel pride. Both men must offer a workable solution to their teams. As in any conflict situation, the workers on both teams are aware of potential conflict. If one leader loses, so does his team, with a likely plunge in morale, productivity, and quality. Pat also recognizes that he can absorb some of the intensity of the feelings by publicly accepting his own responsibility for the work. Then he offers a plan for moving forward.)*

Dave: That new system we saw in Houston?

Pat: Yes, that one. I can get the plans faxed over by this afternoon. Can you guys get together and study them by noon tomorrow? If you think they can work, I'll support the scaffolding construction tomorrow. What do you say?

José: Sure, sounds like a good idea.

Dave: I think so too. I'll be glad to look them over. *(Pat has moved to a consensus—Step 9—reinforcing the importance of collaboration and the need to address the problem head-on. By doing so, he gives both parties an option beyond anger and conflict. To be sure they understand this, he emphasizes the need for action—Step 10.)*

> *Pat:* Good. Because we need to move forward— together. I want your joint opinion by noon tomorrow, at which time I'll decide whether we can use that system or need to find another solution. I know both of you have a heavy workload this afternoon, so I'll let you get back to work. If you need any help, give me a call. If not, I'll see you tomorrow.

Pat wraps the meeting up by setting a clear course of direction and refocusing both parties on the work mission rather than the conflict. If Pat had encountered resistance or an unwillingness on their part to cooperate, he could have adjourned the meeting by saying, "I see we still have some significant differences here. Let's adjourn for now to think about how we can resolve them. I'd like to meet with each of you separately and then together, at which time I'll decide what we will do next."

Workleaders pursue a collaborative but tough-minded process that focuses everyone on the responsibility to fulfill the mission. Exceptional leaders accept the responsibility to manage conflict and risk, and they expect the parties to the conflict to do the same. To conclude Pat's story, the new scaffolding system did work and Dave and José worked closely and effectively to put it in place. Workleaders in our study, like Virginia Siri, get the same sort of results every day.

➤ Protecting the Public and the Corporation— Ginny's Story

Virginia Siri serves as a vice president for Distribution at Johnson & Johnson. She understands J & J not only from the inside out, but from the bottom up, having joined the company fresh out of college as a research assistant in a genetics lab. She soon demonstrated a keen organizational ability and moved onto a leadership development career path. During her training she became fascinated by the process of targeting solutions to customers' needs and volunteered for extensive in-field consumer research. There she identified problems in both product development and distribution, and her experience led the company to ask her to design a system for smoothly connecting the two. She demonstrated such skill that she became head of national distribution operations, a job in which she strove to ensure that the connection between development and distribution of products to the customer was seamless. Throughout Ginny's career, people have turned to her for answers to the toughest problems, so it was no surprise that the company tapped her to deal with its most dangerous crisis.

During the Tylenol tampering scare in the early '80s, Ginny acted as one of the principal architects of a remarkable act of corporate courage and responsibility. At a cost of millions of dollars, Johnson & Johnson recalled all Tylenol capsules from the market following a series of poisonings that involved product package tampering. They acted against the advice of the FBI and the FDA, who both advised J & J to keep the product on the shelf to show that a psychopath could not bring a major corporation to its knees. Wall Street also opposed the recall, which it felt would doom the product forever.

The leaders of J & J, however, felt compelled to address larger issues that neither the FBI nor the FDA had considered. As head of national distribution operations, Ginny was one of the first executives to learn of the emergency. The minute she heard about it, she called an emergency meeting of her distribution leadership team to assess the situation and take charge of it. The results of that meeting went swiftly to the Chair of the Board, who then launched one of the finest efforts to protect the public interest in U.S. corporate history. Ginny and members of her organizational team reconstructed the risk assessment meeting for us. As we join them, they have begun to assess the type of risk they face.

Those present at the meeting, in addition to Ginny, include the national distribution managers for packaging, Oscar Sung; shipping, Niles Cavendish; and customer service, Sharon Zimmerman. We will use the Risk Assessment Guide to follow the proceedings.

Ginny: The news is not good. There's no clue yet as to how, where, and when the poison was introduced. We must assume the worst: that all packaging could be contaminated. What's the risk in this case?

Sharon: Ethical and legal. We're responsible for the welfare of anyone with access to our product.

Oscar: And that's strategic. We know from everyday contact with our customers that they consider J & J to be the one company that stands for integrity and dependability. If we let people down on even this one issue, the whole company could be taken down. Fifty years to build and two weeks to destroy. That's the severity of the risk in my opinion.

Ginny: Oscar, that's pretty intense. Niles and Sharon, do you agree with Oscar that the risk is that high and that urgent?

Niles: Absolutely. If you weren't part of this culture and didn't know how much we've built our whole company on a commitment to public service, you wouldn't realize that trust is our fundamental and far-reaching concern. We either address this issue now or file Chapter 11. Those are the stakes in my opinion. And the boys and girls in the boardroom had better understand that's how real the situation is in the front lines.

Sharon: That raises an immediate need to take action to get the CEO's attention.

Ginny: I already have a call in to him. But before we talk about taking charge in this thing, I want us to nail down the nature of the risk. The CEO team will need a launch point for action, and we're going to give them the plan they need. *(Ginny keeps the group on track, remembering the importance of a rigorous risk assessment in the midst of crisis.)*

Ginny proceeds with the Risk Assessment, anticipating the wide variety of risks that would likely flow from the incident. The group identifies risks in virtually every category listed on the Risk Assessment Guide, which prompts Ginny to raise a fundamental question the group has bypassed until this point.

Ginny: We seem to have identified a full spectrum of risks, which justifies a comprehensive and nationwide intervention. We've failed to address two important questions, however. Where is the risk coming from, and is this a one-shot or long-term problem?

Niles: God only knows who started it or where. It could be one crazy SOB or a fringe group or even some form of state-sponsored terrorism.

Oscar: And, as we said at last year's planning session, once the retail setting becomes a terrorist battleground, it could go on for a long time.

Ginny: I agree. This type of risk is a long-term problem and can come from virtually any source. Regardless of what the FBI ultimately finds out, we must act on the assumption that anyone at any time and place will attack like this. Thus, as we now move to develop a plan to take charge, I want to address the fact that our solution must be comprehensive, not targeted to handle just one or two potential sources or time frames. *(Having assessed the type, level, duration, and source of the risk, Ginny moves the group to the second stage of the process. In this context, she follows the Risk Assessment Guide to the letter.)* Okay, let's take charge of this mess. In light of the risk, what's our objective?

Oscar: First and foremost, get the bad product off the market—now!

Niles: And how do you propose to do that?

Sharon: Well, we could call all our customers and tell them to pull it off the shelves.

Ginny: Hold on a second, everyone. Let's take this in sequence. If our first objective is to pull the product, what's our second objective? *(Ginny retains the discipline of the process. She also realizes that they must develop a full range of objectives to address the full range of risks.)*

Niles: Well, we'd better get good product back out. But I don't know if Oscar's group can handle it.

Oscar: Niles, you just handle your end. I'll take care of mine.

Ginny: Hold on. Let's focus on the objective.

Ginny recognizes that the team is starting to show signs of stress, so she takes decisive steps to manage tension, identifying objectives and ultimately identifying a bold plan for harnessing control and dominating the situation. Ginny's team not only recommends that J & J pull old product from the shelves, but that it put a new tamper-resistant packaging into production immediately. Fortunately, Oscar's group has been experimenting with such packaging for two years. In addition to these actions, Ginny's team recommends one more that ultimately becomes the key to making all the others work.

Ginny:	One more thing. How do we know that this will really work or, more to the point, how our customers will respond?
Sharon:	Ginny, we don't. There's only one way to know, and that's to contact them—all of them. And I'd say we should do it very personally.
Niles:	Sharon, that's impossible. Just send them a letter or take ads out in newspapers across the country. Personal contact's a good idea but impractical.
Sharon:	That's not enough. Our customers need to hear from us directly.
Oscar:	I agree. It's too important to the rest of our plan.
Ginny:	I also agree, and I note that Niles does too in principle. I've been thinking about this type of situation for some time and, after having used teleconferencing as a tool to meet with our staff across the country, I propose that we schedule a series of teleconferences nationwide to explain the plan if it's approved.

Ginny's approach to the Tylenol scare demonstrates the benefit of maintaining discipline in crisis management. Had she not done so, she might never have proposed the use of a relatively new technique of large network teleconferencing. Within 24 hours of her team's recommendations to the Chair of the Board, Ginny and other key executives were scheduled to chair teleconference meetings nationwide with over 2,000 J & J field representatives and key customers.

This bold and responsive act dealt head-on with growing fear in the front lines by making a personal connection that confirmed the company's commitment and responsibility. Each executive followed a specific script and action plan. Ginny memorized it instantly because, almost word for word, it followed the assessment and take-charge plan she and her team had initiated.

Ginny also participated in the corporate postcrisis assessment, which reviewed the company's behavior in the emergency from start to finish. That review led to the permanent incorporation of the Risk Assessment Guide into operational and strategic planning, and the permanent adoption of such techniques as tamper-resistant packaging and teleconferencing, both of which have changed the entire industry. A national poll taken after the crisis revealed that 93 percent of the public admired the way J & J fulfilled its responsibilities to its customers.

Ginny also reported that she used the Conflict Management Guide throughout the crisis, especially to address a conflict between Oscar and Niles that began to erupt during the Risk Assessment process. As Ginny explained, "After we wired our assessment and plan to the chairman, I asked each member of the team to join me individually for a conference. There I discovered that Niles was angry at Oscar for failing to consider the shipping and handling problems he would have in dealing with both the removal of the old product and replacement with new packaging. Oscar, by contrast, was completely absorbed in finding a solution to the packaging challenge and was unaware of Niles' concerns. I brought them both together, and had them share their different perspectives. Then we discussed the fact that the mission would be lost if either failed to serve the other. They agreed and quickly became the closest of colleagues. In fact, all of us became tremendously close. I attribute that to the discipline of honoring everyone as individuals by meeting with them independently and together every day during the crisis. I used the Conflict Management Guide to keep us together."

Anyone can behave well when the water remains calm and the winds blow favorably, but when storms strike and crises threaten organizations, only the most disciplined of leaders can keep their steady hands on the helm. The tools Ginny used not only enabled a major corporation to weather an unexpected storm, they helped calm the waters and eventually made the whole organization stronger. Crisis will attack, and when it does, workleaders armed with tools for disciplined risk assessment and conflict management will steer their organizations toward ever-higher levels of achievement.

■ FULFILLING THE ROLE OF THE PROTECTOR

The motto for America's armed forces, "To Serve and Protect," applies to each and every workleader in our study. During an era when it has become fashionable to adopt cut and run strategies during crisis, our workleaders demonstrate the very opposite behavior. Rather than avoiding risk and the threat of crisis, they embrace them as opportunities to demonstrate their own worth and to protect those they serve.

Recognizing that all of life's activities entail risk and that the most ambitious missions invite the greatest challenges, workleaders accept responsibility to manage inevitable crises with the discipline embodied in the Risk Assessment and Conflict Management Guides. Like the war chants of Native American warriors, these guides preserve one's identity and mission by distilling the timeless lessons of battle. As we'll see in the Chapter 9: The Synergizer, such preparation makes it possible to transform an organization or nation from an object buffeted by fate and chance into an irresistible force for achievement.

9
The Synergizer

He was a synergizer—an architect, farmer, engineer, and scholar, as well as an attorney and statesman—who drew on many talents and skills to create a whole greater than the sum of its parts. In 1769, at the age of 26, he performed his first important act of service when he supported a motion before the House of Burgesses for the emancipation of slaves.

He was an eloquent writer. As a member of the Third Congress he accepted the chairmanship of a committee charged with drafting a declaration of independence on which 13 American colonies could act to sever their subservience to Great Britain. On July 4, 1776, Congress accepted that declaration essentially as submitted. It began: "We hold these truths to be self-evident, that all men are created equal, that they are endowed by their Creator with certain unalienable Rights, that among these are Life, Liberty, and the pursuit of Happiness."

He was Thomas Jefferson, and his work and words have transcended the time and place in which he lived to create a whole greater than the sum of its parts that infused an entire nation with an optimism and dedication to equality that still serves as its bedrock of belief.

One of his less well-known accomplishments was the drafting of another pivotal document in the history of the United States, the Virginia Statute for Religious Freedom, enacted in 1786. This landmark document articulated Jefferson's belief in every individual's right and ability to choose personal beliefs wisely. It spurred him to write, "Whereas Almighty God hath created the free mind . . . to compel a man to furnish contributions of money for the propagation of opinions which he disbelieves is sinful and tyrannical; . . . truth is great and will prevail. . . ."

Jefferson practiced all the roles of the workleader throughout his 40 years of public service as a member of Congress, governor of Virginia, foreign minister, Vice President and President of the United States, and founder of the University of Virginia. He selected wisely, connected ardently, solved problems adroitly, evaluated judiciously, negotiated shrewdly, healed relentlessly, and protected vigorously, and in so doing he became a true synergizer, the effect of whose actions is greater than the sum of those actions.

He would have understood the motto, "Every leader works and every worker leads." Though a brilliant scholar, statesman, and writer, whose work in political science, history, and the physical sciences won wide acclaim in Europe as well as America, Jefferson devoted himself equally to practical affairs. As an architect, he designed the University of Virginia and his lovely home, Monticello. He learned the art of clockmaking from his friend David Rittenhouse, the famed clockmaker of Philadelphia. He designed folding doors, a circular filing cabinet for his music, a revolving chair, the first dumbwaiter in America, a new type of plow that functioned more effectively than any other in use at the time, and myriad other devices. He worked.

At the same time he led, inspired by a deep and abiding faith in the ability of the rank and file to govern themselves wisely. His faith in the capacity of individuals to set and achieve worthy goals and in the importance of education in achieving these goals is revealed in the simple epitaph he wrote for his own tombstone: "Here lies Thomas Jefferson, Author of the American Declaration of Independence, of the

Statute of Virginia for Religious Freedom, and the Father of the University of Virginia."

▣ THE ROLE OF THE SYNERGIZER

Like Jefferson, the workleaders in this chapter—Leo Lopez, Anita Jones, and Sam Walton—fulfilled the role of the synergizer, an overarching responsibility that unites and frames all the others we identified in our study. The synergizer achieves a concert of skills in which the interplay of disciplines brings associates and leaders to a higher level of accomplishment than they could have achieved otherwise. Like a Beethoven symphony, the synergizer provides a larger structure within which individuals and teams come together to achieve a whole greater than the sum of its parts.

The skills and scripts of the synergizer result from *and* provide a baseline for the other roles of the workleader. The synergizer knows that regardless of the scope of an individual's responsibility, the process of human progress remains the same—analyzing and making choices, then putting those choices into practice. Deeply pragmatic, workleaders believe that they must demonstrate the principles and practices they preach. Regardless of how lofty their vision or ideals, workleaders translate their beliefs into a process of living that empowers their people to take control of their own destiny.

Through the role of the synergizer, workleaders impress the principles of self-determination and its corollary, personal responsibility, deeply into the consciousness of their organizations. This reflects the seminal characteristic of the 1,029 exceptional leaders identified by both colleagues and customers in our study population of more than 18,000 people.

Workleaders believe that recognition and success hinge on what they know and what they can personally achieve.

They and the people they choose and who choose them have renounced the two inauthentic types of leaders that so dominate the daily news: the celebrity leaders—who believe that who they know and how well they're known should be the keys to advancement, and the money leaders—who believe that money and the drive for the power it represents offer the keys to success. While workleaders receive recognition and wield a good deal of influence, they prize their competence and ability to contribute above any personal glory or power to control or buy others.

Backed by their absolute commitment to a process of open exploration and decision making, workleaders possess confidence in their own abilities to compete effectively and recognize that only the ability to serve the welfare of the customer and community affords them personal success. This places them in direct opposition to the new elitism of celebrity leaders, who attempt to control access to opportunity by establishing selection criteria based on whom they know and their social, economic, and academic pedigree, and money leaders, who simply block access to power by buying it.

Workleaders prove remarkably creative and adaptive in overcoming such contemporary obstacles to achievement. They break through the circle of celebrity to connect with the larger community by respecting customers' and frontline workers' influence and by recognizing accomplishment. Pragmatic thinkers, they are driven by an intense commitment to serve. As a result, they instinctively inhabit the front lines of service to find opportunities to achieve rather than hide in the rear lines of privilege as observers.

Like Jefferson, these contemporary pluralists believe that the democratic give and take of open debate and commerce wins them the best hope of progress. They understand that the noble ideals of the Declaration of Independence actually provide a common-sense blueprint for individual success, which they have adapted into a synergistic process of managing change. In this chapter we have organized this process into two tools: the *Choices for Change* and the *Seven-Step Guide to Self-Improvement*. The following overview sums up the role of the synergizer.

THE ROLE OF THE SYNERGIZER

Goal: Create a whole greater than the sum of its parts
Method: The Synergizer Process

➤ Diagnose Choices for Change with Tool #1.
  • Synergy
  • Entropy
  • Feel good change
  • Crisis-driven change

➤ Use Tool #2: The Seven-Step Guide to Self-Improvement.
  • Establish context
  • Measure mission effectiveness
  • Identify opportunities
  • Mobilize support
  • Take action
  • Evaluate results
  • Improve continuously

The visionary articulates an idea, the strategist designs a plan for action, and the tactician devises methods of implementation. Synergizers, however, do all three and more simultaneously, harnessing the force of change to transport people to a higher state of achievement. The new path to the future they choose follows a logical step-wise progression, moving from an abstract promise of progress to a practical script for everyday living. This script bonds hope and reason through an ever-strengthening energy field of commitment to produce a synergistic breakthrough of insight and resolve.

The immortal documents that Jefferson drafted synthesized the concepts of scientific inquiry and free thought that had been advancing since the Renaissance into a new rationale for government based on self-determination. His ideas also provide leaders with action plans for mobilizing a diverse group of people. Those action plans have helped shape the evolution of civilization since 1776, and they still influence people in every corner of the globe. The new and more open world economy testifies not only to the force of Jefferson's thinking and the depth of his insight but also to his ability to transform ideas into scripts for action.

Our study revealed a remarkable insight: Synergizers plant the seeds for the future by achieving in the present. They dig deeply into the operational realities of their organizations, help people accomplish all that they can possibly accomplish today, and then help them top their full potential to accomplish even more tomorrow. It all comes down to the right vision, strategy, and tactics for harnessing change.

➤ Tool #1: Diagnosing Choices for Change

Since workleaders know that change is the only constant in the sea of variables that affect success, they take the initiative and choose pathways for change. Those who wait for change are usually surprised by it, if not downright battered by it. Rather than sitting idly by while change exacts its toll, workleaders seek ways to anticipate, adapt, or even invent change. The *Choices for Change* chart classifies four types of change and the ways in which individuals, teams, and organizations deal with them. The chart shows a variety of responses to change. The first is *entropy,* where the fear of change causes paralysis and passivity. This avoidance and denial of reality typically lead to serious disconnection. Another reaction to change is the *feel good* response. Individuals who pursue feel good change behave in an accommodating fashion, submitting to a safe course of action and ultimately realizing little benefit from change. A third type of change is *crisis-driven,* characterized by hostility, defiance, and overreaction. Finally comes *synergistic* change, where a vision of the future is inte-

Tool #1: Choices for Change

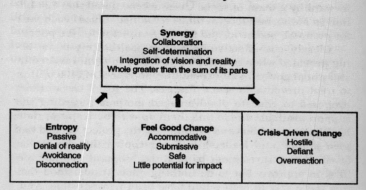

Synergy
Collaboration
Self-determination
Integration of vision and reality
Whole greater than the sum of its parts

Entropy	Feel Good Change	Crisis-Driven Change
Passive	Accommodative	Hostile
Denial of reality	Submissive	Defiant
Avoidance	Safe	Overreaction
Disconnection	Little potential for impact	

grated with reality to find new ways to achieve a whole greater than the sum of its parts through collaboration and self-determination.

Workleaders use Choices for Change to help them understand change and move more deliberately to anticipate, actively adapt to, and invent change.

➤ A Script for Choosing Change

Leo Lopez, a senior vice president in the investment banking firm of Donaldson, Lufkin and Jenrette (DLJ) faced a dilemma as he reviewed a proposal for an unusual new venture. As a nationally recognized healthcare CEO and public service policymaker, he had been recruited by DLJ to head its rapidly growing public financing operation, which included such governmental projects as the multibillion-dollar atomic collider project near Dallas and the financing of healthcare reform. During a review of various proposals for the latter, Leo weighed a venture to provide greater healthcare access to the disadvantaged and poor. The proposal, put forward by a team of social caseworkers, noted that $20 billion in authorized federal funds remained unused each year for prenatal, pediatric, and family healthcare for the poor.

Clearly, cost-effective preventive healthcare was not being provided when it could be, and this, in turn, resulted in an annual government expenditure in excess of $100 billion to treat preventable acute illnesses. The social caseworkers proposed to educate disadvantaged mothers regarding the support available and to link them up with both appropriate healthcare providers and funding. All the project needed was seed money and leadership. Leo recounts the choices he faced: "As an investment banker, the proposal was just too 'iffy' to approve. But to do nothing once I understood that this was a way to help would have been irresponsible. And, on yet another hand, to pass the proposal on to others for venture funding when I knew it needed improvement would have consigned it to a slow death. And to have turned it over to the public offering group would have invited ridicule and hostility. There was only one real choice given the gravity of the challenge and the chance to make a contribution. I took leave of DLJ and financed it myself."

Synergizers act as catalysts to harness forces for change and lead people forward. Lopez analyzed the choices for change, and he chose. He formed Eligibility Services, Inc., one of America's most respected new corporations, which is pioneering healthcare access for America's poor. Leo has been able to link patients and healthcare providers by accessing previously unused funds in excess of $5 billion, saving federal and state governments over $20 billion that would otherwise have been spent on acute medical emergencies.

Leo, like other workleaders, evaluated his choices for change and chose the path of collaborative self-determination, empowering those who lacked options with the ability to take control of an important part of their lives. By using the Choices for Change diagnostic chart, any workleader can set the stage to launch a comprehensive self-improvement process.

➤ Tool #2: The Seven-Step Guide to Self-Improvement

Workleaders incorporated Choices for Change with a seven-step process of continuous self-improvement. This synergistic process provides the overarching framework within which they fulfill all their other roles. Each of the other seven roles provides scripts to address specific situations that arise as people learn to tap into the power of change through a continuous process of self-improvement. Workleaders view change as an ever-present tidal force for progress while average leaders try to erect bulwarks against change. By harnessing change, workleaders help people gather the momentum necessary to achieve synergistic breakthroughs of insight and collective resolve. The following chart summarizes the seven steps workleaders follow in implementing change.

Change management begins by taking action to first reduce the fear and anxiety that always accompany change, and then reduce the complexity of change to manageable levels. Tool #1: Choices for Change does just that because it establishes a context for action that defines the challenge and promotes a vision for meeting it. Stakeholders need a context to understand why they should work together as a unified team and a mission that enables them to focus their commitment. By establishing a context for action, workleaders prevent destructive and time-consuming arguments over assigning responsibility or blame for change. Instead they move their associates directly to Step 2, where they can assess the organization's overall mission effectiveness and its ability to manage change.

Workleaders realize they need to weigh the severity of the challenge in terms of the risk it represents to the organization's vision, including the organization's values and its stakeholders' aspirations. The central question in such an assessment asks whether associates are positioned for change: "Are the right people in the right place, at the right time, for the right reason and cost to achieve the mission?"

TOOL #2: THE SEVEN-STEP GUIDE TO SELF-IMPROVEMENT

Step 1: Establish context.
Action: Define the challenge and the vision for meeting it.
Objective: Unify the organization and develop self-confidence and commitment.
Risk: Other esteem: Searching for purpose and identity outside the organization.
Lesson: Stakeholders must know who they are as a team and why they should work together.

Step 2: Measure mission effectiveness.
Action: Undertake an organizationwide global assessment: Are the right people in the right place at the right time, for the right reason and cost to achieve the mission?
Objective: Own and experience reality.
Risk: Failure to understand the consequences of *not* meeting the challenge.
Lesson: Overcome fear and resistance to change by immersing stakeholders in the organization's reality.

Step 3: Identify opportunities for improvement.
Action: Use data to identify actionable opportunities for improvement.
Objective: Develop a data-driven plan for action.
Risk: Failure to set practical, achievable targets that build strength and confidence.
Lesson: Stakeholders will understand how to change when they understand the reasons for it.

Step 4: Mobilize support.
Action: Share the plan.
Objective: Enfold those who are ready for change.
Risk: Wasting energy on those who refuse to change.
Lesson: Build a magnet of positivism by focusing on those who are ready to change.

Step 5: Take action.
Action: Implement the plan.
Objective: Honor those who serve by involving them in their own transformation.
Risk: Attempting to do too much and thus achieving little.
Lesson: The more radical and far-reaching the agenda for action, the more it must be tempered by moderation.

Step 6: Measure results.
Action: Measure success and failure.
Objective: Grow and mature from start-up visionaries to seasoned achievers.
Risk: Focusing on the present and failing to identify the risks and opportunities ahead.
Lesson: By measuring results, leaders strengthen their legitimacy and stakeholders' commitment to the vision.

Step 7: Improve continuously.
Action: Repeat the seven-step process.
Objective: Build tenacity and create a synergistic kick of insight and energy.
Risk: Loss of momentum; unwillingness to sustain the process feeds cynicism and destroys leadership credibility.
Lesson: Nothing succeeds like persistence.

This ultimate question should occupy any person or group of people facing a new reality. Workleaders realize that failure to undertake such an assessment will result in failure to fulfill their leadership responsibilities. Just as a surgical team needs to know the diagnostic results of lab work and x-rays to assess the risks of surgery, associates need to know how efficiently and effectively the organization as a whole and its individual members are performing. Such an assessment helps reduce skepticism and cynicism while stressing the practical admonition "In God we trust; all others must use data." Assessment helps the team to own the new reality and, with that sense of ownership, overcome fear of the unknown.

An understanding of present performance makes it possible to take Step 3 and identify opportunities for improvement. In a democratic culture such as the one Jefferson envisioned, free people will not meekly submit to a leader's mandate if they don't believe or understand it. They require verifiable data to set practical, achievable targets for change. A data-driven plan helps stakeholders understand how they should act in order to effect measurable improvement.

With context, assessment, and plan in hand, move to mobilize support—Step 4—creating a magnet of positivism for change. Rigorously preparing people for change helps them get behind the program with great gusto. The leader concentrates on those who are ready to change, providing them with an achievable agenda for taking action—Step 5.

From the instant action is initiated, workleaders prepare to evaluate results—Step 6. Periodically, those who practice learned optimism rigorously prepare for the possibility of failure, because by doing so they radically reduce the odds that failure will occur. Workleaders view evaluation as a risk management activity that offers the opportunity for timely and thus less traumatic course correction. They recognize that the act of evaluation strengthens commitment and the willingness to improve, which in turn sustains the momentum of self-determination and commitment to continuous improvement—Step 7.

Through this seven-step process, workleaders develop the capacity to generate one synergistic kick of progress after another. This phenomenon has propelled the growth of Microsoft, Intel, and, as we'll see, Wal-Mart. It enabled the leadership team at West Jersey Health System to propel their organization forward during an era of dramatic transformational change in healthcare.

➤ Creating a Synergistic Kick — West Jersey's Script for Change

West Jersey Health System, located just across the Walt Whitman Bridge from Philadelphia, has consistently honored the tradition of community service and represents the very best of the United States' commitment to providing state-of-the-art healthcare close to home. Recognizing that this tradition and the deeply committed team of 5,000 caregivers who make up West Jersey's workforce could become casualties in the often predatory managed care marketplace, the senior leadership team embarked on a comprehensive seven-step self-improvement process to take control of their own destiny. The following script outlines how they took each step. Listen as Chief Executive Officer Richard Miller, Chief Operating Officer Kevin Manley, systemwide Redesign Process Chair Anita Jones, and Division Heads Joan Meyers and Jim Shedno review their first year's effort.

Step 1: Establish Context — Define the Challenge and the Vision for Meeting It

Rich: While politicians, reformers, insurance companies, and consultants claim to know how to restructure healthcare from the outside in, we know that real change must come from the inside out—

from the deep reservoir of commitment that our associates have for our patients. In approaching our situation, we knew that if we waited passively, we'd entropy. We also knew we couldn't pursue microlevel or incremental change, which is what often happens with so-called Total Quality Management. And we sure didn't want to subject our people and our patients to the type of irresponsible, angry change often called *radical reengineering*. We needed to build on the greatest strength of our organization—our people—and collaboratively redesign and unify our operations at a new level of focus.

Joan: We evaluated our choice of futures and decided we'd write our own Declaration of Independence.

Kevin: Right, and to do it we knew we had to get all of our associates on board. So, we prepared a State of the System Report on the challenges we faced, presented it to the board, the community and all of our associates . . .

Jim: And then we asked everyone in the organization to assess our readiness.

Rich: Yes, but before we explain that, we need to emphasize that we offered the State of the System analysis as a hypothesis. We wanted to educate our people, not dictate to them. We wanted everyone ready to join us in thinking the situation through. So, we found out the facts: the government's slashing of reimbursement, the pressure from HMOs to make money, the public's uneasiness and the tremendous fear among our patients and even our workforce. We put the cards on the table and, like a good clinician talking to a patient, we said, "Let's join together to meet this challenge head-on."

Anita: That's what made the assessment work. We prepared our people, and gave them a context that defined the challenge and a vision for meeting it, which was to work together honestly and openly.

Step 2: Measure Mission Effectiveness—Are the Right People in the Right Place at the Right Time, for the Right Reason and Cost to Achieve the Mission?

Kevin: And, as we explained the context, we asked everyone to participate in a very unusual and far-reaching assessment. You know, when a patient's symptoms suggest heart or lung disease, we take them right in for an in-depth diagnosis—an MRI, blood work-up, EKG, the works. We believed the same was necessary for our organization.

Joan: We said we were going to treat our organization as if it were a patient and do the most thorough work-up you could imagine.

Anita: We created internal consulting teams to work with our managers and staff and asked every single person to examine what they did, its time and cost, and the roadblocks that got in the way of doing the job right. We told everyone that we, not outsiders, were going to evaluate whether "the right people were in the right place for the right cost to carry out our mission." We used a new technology called Work Imaging to do this and it helped us see that thirty to forty percent of all labor dollars were being spent overcoming roadblocks and coping with inefficient systems, territorial blockages, departmental duplication, and, most importantly, complexity and overlap between individual roles.

Rich: It was both a humbling and gratifying experience. We looked at ourselves and evaluated the
challenge honestly and openly. Regardless of
their role in the organization, our people demonstrated remarkable courage and commitment.

Step 3: Identify Opportunities for Improvement— Use Data to Identify Actionable Opportunities for Improvement

Jim: The most powerful part of this was when we
looked at the data for opportunities to change.
No group of people on earth is more skeptical
and sophisticated when it comes to data than
physicians, nurses, and healthcare providers in
general. But when they looked at the data that
they had generated about the way we actually do
things, they believed. We had fancy statistics and
benchmarks, but because we had done the assessment ourselves, we didn't need them to smell,
feel, and touch the challenge. It was real.

Anita: One example makes this point. Professionals like
nurses, pharmacists, lab techs, and respiratory
therapists are paranoid over the possibility of
losing their jobs. Well, when they saw that over
forty percent of all professional work overlapped
with support staff and could have been done by
support staff, they knew that things must change.
They saw professional selfishness and knew that
it was a disservice to the patient and to their colleagues. Not only were professionals losing focus
on what they should have been doing, but they
were taking jobs away from support staff by
doing work that could have been delegated to
them.

Joan: As a nurse myself, I knew immediately when I saw those figures that we had to redesign all the jobs in our system to increase our professional focus on the patient.

Jim: That was one of many opportunities that we identified. We also saw that we had to streamline processes like scheduling transportation and documentation. And we also had to streamline management.

Step 4: Mobilize Support—Share the Plan

Kevin: And here is where real growth occurs. We took this diagnosis and, just like a physician shares a diagnosis with the patient, we shared it with our whole community, all the people we had spoken with initially.

Joan: We identified opportunities and mobilized for action by forming cross-functional teams made up of people from across the system representing all ranks. We believe that if you can live with the reality of serving a seriously ill patient, you deserve the chance to participate in your own survival.

Anita: We also gave all our managers their own data to examine and taught them how to undertake a redesign analysis. It seems that managers are taught everything but how to manage the work. They deserve a fighting chance to succeed in a world that's been turned on its head.

Jim: Yes, we know that there will be thirty to forty percent fewer managers in healthcare in five years. But eighty percent of the leaders we will need are right here. We owe it to our patients to develop this wonderful pool of talent.

Step 5: Take Action—Implement the Plan

> Kevin: After we fed the diagnosis and plan back, we
> went right to work. Just last week the team look-
> ing at role complexity and overlap gave us a plan
> that would change virtually every clinical profes-
> sional's portfolio of work. It would refocus them
> more clearly on why they're here. We're now
> preparing to implement that plan by offering
> people the chance to apply for those new roles. It
> will mean streamlining, but then we asked our
> people what they thought: Ninety percent said
> they knew it was the right thing to do for our
> patients, even if it meant some of their jobs
> would be lost and virtually everybody's job would
> change.

> Rich: Ninety percent! When people tell me front-line
> people won't face reality, I tell them they need to
> do an arrogance check. People who work for a liv-
> ing and who try to honor the principles of this
> culture are ready for change. It's leadership—the
> pretentious and the powerful—who don't get it.
> This plan will improve the quality of our ser-
> vice—which is already excellent—and save over
> twenty-five million dollars. By following this pro-
> cess of self-improvement, we're already achieving
> synergies we never saw before.

Steps 6 and 7: Measure Results and Improve
Continuously—Measure Success and Failure
and Repeat the Seven-Step Process

> Kevin: As we evaluate our process through another cycle
> of Work Imaging, I can only see our people get-
> ting more determined and focused. It's been

truly a privilege to be part of this team. It's getting stronger and stronger each day.

One of the most revealing aspects of this conversation with the team of West Jersey workleaders was how fluently they present a script for implementing the seven-step process. They have developed a remarkable synergy as a team, keying into each others' thoughts and motivations to create a collective consciousness and resolve that is far greater than any one of them could have projected alone. The remarkable synergies of service and savings being achieved at West Jersey prove the extraordinary ability of workleaders to propel their organizations forward by achieving synergistic kicks of insight, energy, and focus.

On a very practical level, this conversation also illustrates the power of a script for change, whether addressing individual or systemwide change, or whether it involves microscale change or major transformational change. From Rich and the senior leadership team to the very front lines of service, associates at West Jersey learned how to play a part in the organization's script for change. Workleaders from Thomas Jefferson to Abraham Lincoln to Sam Walton, our final workleader example, understood that leadership is fundamentally an act of providing people with scripts to manage change and harness the synergistic potential in their lives.

The average leaders in our study generally share the misconception that the management of large-scale change should remain in the hands of only the very top or elite level of the organization. As we've emphasized throughout this book, workleaders believe and practice the very opposite strategy, translating concepts and plans at the macrolevel into concrete scripts for living in the front lines. By contrast, the leadership principles advocated by average leaders reveal an underlying condescension toward those who do work in the front lines of service. Ironically, only front-line workers, as Rich and Kevin noted, will determine the ultimate success or failure of any change effort. No one knew this better than Sam Walton, founder of Wal-Mart and one of our most intriguing workleaders.

➤ A Script for Synergizing an Organization— Mr. Sam's Story

At the time of his death in April, 1994, "Mr. Sam," as Wal-Mart's 300,000 associates called their founder Sam Walton, had built the most successful retail business in American history. While that fact alone would have satisfied most CEOs, Mr. Sam didn't use such a conventional measure of success. He was a man who at the peak of his corporate life still spent most of his time personally flying his twin-engine plane on store-hopping campaigns to meet with people in the front lines of service. He was a man with a cause whose life's satisfaction came from more than a healthy bottom line.

Mr. Sam wrote a "Declaration of Independence" releasing the customer from the yoke of Madison Avenue oppression and corporate price gouging. With his wife Helen, who convinced him that working women represented the most powerful consumer force in American economic life, he dedicated himself to proving that the customer could function as a fully vested partner in commerce through a strategy that paid the customer back for assuming self-service and product education responsibilities. He turned the concept of *sale* on its head, and with it the haggling and deceit of the bazaar, by offering "everyday low prices." The movement he spawned reduced gross profit margins in the industry from over 60 percent in the 1950s to 22 percent in the 1990s—all of which, he explained, provided greater access to goods and services for those who needed them the most.

Mr. Sam personified the synergistic workleader. When we asked Wal-Mart associates to identify the most effective and trustworthy leaders they knew, they mentioned Sam Walton 10 to 1 over any other person in the organization. Their vote did not reflect an abstract assessment. To people like George in Berryville, Arkansas, Sam Walton was a flesh-and-blood associate, someone who made things happen: "Mr. Sam visited here often. The first time, he called me on my performance on customer satisfaction and taught me how to overcome my shyness and key into people's needs. Then he came again, and again, and checked on my progress, teaching me how to read my financials. He didn't just talk about leading; he was there, right with you even when he became the wealthiest man in the U.S."

Sam Walton could define a challenge and create a vision for meeting it in a way that galvanized people to perform at extraordinary levels of intensity and focus. Like Jefferson, Leo, and the team at West Jersey, he created a context in which the whole became larger than the sum of its parts. In an industry that had initially treated employees as interchangeable and disposable, he provided ownership and profit sharing, and in a field where "customer beware" had always ruled the day, he built trust and loyalty through unparalleled access to information and protection of customer rights. Finally, in a field where the hustle for a buck can diminish the value of human effort, he created commitment that connected a modest collection of variety stores into the largest and most cohesive retail empire in the world, with revenues in excess of $50 billion.

Through interviews with his associates and with Mr. Sam himself, we gained insight into Sam Walton the synergizer. In addition to Mr. Sam, Tucky Wesley from Wilkesboro, North Carolina; Atti "The Colonel" Prekub from Texarkana, Arkansas; and Sol Lowenheim from Birmingham, Alabama, explained this synergy to us in no uncertain terms.

Step 1: Establish Context

Mr. Sam: Helen said she wouldn't live in a town of more than 10,000. If we kept our roots in small-town America, we wouldn't lose our sense of what free choice and self-reliance meant. If we lived these values ourselves, we'd be more likely to honor them in our customers.

Atti: Mr. Sam said the challenge was to constantly find ways to give the customers more value and control over their lives. He was especially concerned about working women who needed a place they could trust to give them the best product for the best price. They don't have the time to worry about being cheated and Mr. Sam said they'd be loyal to us if we treated them with the dignity and respect we would like to receive ourselves.

Sol: He was a practical philosopher who could have been anything he wanted. He couldn't stand the fame game or the money game— except as it helped him reach out further. In the early days he mortgaged everything but his kids to put his ideas into practice. Money didn't drive him, but the thought that he could make a difference for people did.

Tucky: Mr. Walton, as I called him, had an extraordinarily precise vision of what he wanted and how we all could benefit from helping to get there. As he got older, he shared more and more, not out of any guilt but because he realized that people would give more than they received. To me, he's an example of what democracy and opportunity are all about.

Sam Walton established a clear context for all his people that carries over to this day. He defined the challenge as one of customer value and self-control, and the vision as self-service and everyday low prices. Sam Walton could easily translate such ideas into concrete terms that everyone could understand and act on. This made it possible to institute what is arguably his greatest operational practice. By setting a clear context he could hold everyone accountable to it by implementing continuous measurement of mission focus. Mr. Sam turned every associate into an evaluator by sharing financial and customer satisfaction information more openly than anyone in business history. As a result, he mentored an empowered workforce that knows how to make course corrections before a situation becomes a serious threat to survival.

Step 2: Measure Mission Effectiveness

Atti: I've become an entrepreneur and businesswoman because of Mr. Sam. He personally showed me why I needed to know about margins and customer satisfaction. He showed me how to turn my department into a profitable opportunity to earn bonuses and buy stock. That gave me real, not pretend, rewards. But my point is that it's all in whether you'll measure the results and hold yourself accountable.

Sol: Sam was a genius at distributing power to the people closest to the customer. By teaching them how to evaluate financial and service performance he created a workforce that has forced everybody to open up and play by the same rules. It seems simple, but when you're held responsible to make the measure, you hold the whole company responsible, which improves everyone's performance.

A lot of consultants talk about the need for personal and organizational accountability, but Sam Walton actually gave his people the tools they needed to measure their performance and hold themselves accountable for results.

Step 3: Identify Opportunities for Improvement

Mr. Sam: I want everybody to know how this business operates. We share more information than anybody and it shows. Our margins are twice as good as Sears' and our return on equity has been more than twenty-five percent per year. Our people know about return on floor space and return on service. This equips them to spot trouble before it gets too far and to suggest opportunities to improve all the time.

Tucky: Finding better ways to do things is just a way of life. It's all because we get information on our performance all the time. It prods you into finding ways to do better.

The obsession with improvement has become legendary at Wal-Mart. In one of the classic stories of improvement, a marketing student named Steven Schulteis came up with a way to cut expenses when he was working in distribution. Wal-Mart's practice had been to use different boxes to separate items by department when filling orders from stores. Schulteis showed how this practice was not only inefficient but led to crushed boxes and the purchasing of an unnecessary number of boxes. He simply proposed putting materials from different departments in the same box. When the plan went into effect it produced a ten percent savings on packaging and an average annual savings of $600,000 per store. In addition to giving him a job, Wal-Mart established a scholarship in Steve's name to honor his suggestion and recognize the dominant role continuous improvement plays in the company's culture.

Mr. Sam:	That's a trademark of ours. We are always willing to change. This business changes all the time and you need to stay flexible. Our people are smart and know what the customer wants. I want them to try anything they think will work. It might not work, but many ideas do, and when they do they're terrific.

Step 4: Mobilize Support

Perhaps Mr. Sam's most famous quirk was his knack of showing up at a store without more than an hour's notice. While such a practice may seem like grandstanding to an outsider, it represented a core value to Walton and his associates and is a key to understanding how he mobilized his people to such high levels of effectiveness.

Mr. Sam:	The most important thing I do is get out to the stores. It's tough work and I want our associates to know I understand, I've been there, and I'll be there as long as I can be.
Tucky:	You understand why you're here because Mr. Walton is there. This can be a tough, dreary business but it can also give you a real sense of achievement. He makes that evident by his presence and shows us we can accomplish things like he has.

Steps 5, 6, and 7: Take Action, Measure Results, and Improve Continuously

Mr. Sam:	The most important difference between us and other stores, such as Kmart, is that we train our people to be merchants. We show

our people all the numbers so they know
how they're doing within the store and the
company. We build responsibility and commitment that way and give people a chance
to do something important with their lives.
We share the profits, the ownership, and the
future. It's one of the best things I've ever
done.

Sam Walton was a genius at setting context, measuring
results, identifying opportunities, and mobilizing people to
action. As a result, he built one of the most resilient organizational cultures in U.S. business and institutionalized the
ideas of action, evaluation, and continuous improvement
into the daily work practices of virtually every associate.

■ FULFILLING THE ROLE OF THE SYNERGIZER

The common threads of values and discipline that weave
through the stories of Jefferson, Lopez, West Jersey, and Walton help to explain their extraordinary levels of achievement. Their values enriched their discipline, which tapped
their powers of reason and resolve, resulting in a synergy of
wills that propelled both individuals and organizations to
breakthrough levels of insight and accomplishment.

The role of the synergizer captures this process of large-
scale transformation in a practical Seven-Step Guide to Self-
Improvement. The guide addresses the visionary, strategic,
and tactical objectives of leadership in a way that integrates
large-scale change with everyday life. For a workleader,
change is a seamless spiral from selection, connection, problem solving, evaluation, negotiation, healing, and protection to the culminating act of synergizing. This continuity
of practice lies at the heart of the workleader's integrity and
power to attain incomparable levels of achievement.

E. C. Murphy, Ltd.

The Leadership IQ Self-Assessment

A COMPREHENSIVE DEVELOPMENTAL ASSESSMENT FOR INDIVIDUALS SEEKING TO IDENTIFY OPPORTUNITIES FOR SELF-IMPROVEMENT IN BOTH WORK AND PERSONAL LIFE

■ INTRODUCTION

We have designed the Leadership IQ (LIQ) Self-Assessment to help leaders gain a basic overview of their present levels of accomplishment with respect to the guiding principles and skills embodied in the Eight Roles of Intelligent Leadership.

The self-assessment employs scenarios based on the scripts that benchmark workleaders use every day. Our workleader research revealed that these scripts and the traditional strategies and tools they employ often defy intuition and conventional logic. In other words, they often challenge traditional thought processes. Sometimes the scripts differ only subtly from conventional practice, but even slight differences can greatly influence outcomes, reaffirming the research on evolutionary survival that demonstrates the profound impact that, over time, slight advantages can have in producing dramatically different results.

As you apply the self-assessment, look for these slight but significant differences as well as for more dramatic ones. Following the self-assessment you will find a development guide that will help you target your reading to achieve maximum results. In addition to focusing on specific areas for improvement as revealed by the LIQ Self-Assessment, you will benefit from reading the whole book in sequence to reinforce the continuity of the lessons and the synergistic kick that you can achieve through competency in all the roles of intelligent leadership.

➤ Directions

The LIQ Self-Assessment presents possible solutions to specific scenarios. Read each scenario and, *right on the assessment itself, circle one of the three choices offered.* After completing the assessment, compare your answers to the answer key provided. The key will reveal your present overall Leadership IQ and help you target areas for improvement.

Consult the Development Guide to find specific sections of the book that explain the logic behind the best choice.

1. You are the Chief Operating Officer for a medium-sized computer technology company, and you have decided to terminate the employment of Bruce, one of your managers. He is considered rude by your customers and is not well respected by his subordinates. And to top it all off, his department's performance has been steadily worsening over the past ten months. You have tried on numerous occasions to help him understand and correct his behavior, but nothing has worked. Finally, after evaluation and counseling have failed, you decide to fire him. You call him into your office for the termination interview, and say the following:

   a. "Bruce, we need to discuss your separation from the company. We've discussed your performance numerous times over the past several months and there has been little improvement. Thus, it would be best for all parties if we went our separate ways. Stop by personnel on your way out to complete all of the appropriate paperwork and pick up your last check."

   b. "Bruce, I've asked you in to discuss your separation from the company. We've discussed your performance numerous times over the past several months and there has been little improvement. I'm not sure if it's the situation here or what. I feel that we had agreed upon attainable goals and they haven't been reached in a timely fashion."

c. "Bruce, over the past several months I think I've been pretty fair with you. I've tried to help you improve and become a team player, but you just haven't listened to me. I'm beginning to wonder if maybe there is really a deeper problem here. Our customers think you're rude, no one on your team really reacts well to you, and I just don't think you're going to cut it as a manager in this industry."

2. You've recently been promoted to head the sales division for a large pharmaceutical company. Bob Jones, the company's top salesperson for the past 20 years, seems to be going through a tough time. His sales have fallen way off, and he doesn't seem as excited about his job as he once was. You decide you need to find some way to reengage him and help him turn his performance around. You invite him to lunch and after some polite small talk you say:

a. "Bob, you have an excellent record at PharmTech, which makes your recent sales figures all the more striking. Would you mind, though, if we set that issue aside for a moment and talked about a more basic question—namely, you? Where are you with things? How do you feel about your job, your customers, and your relationship with PharmTech?"

b. "Bob, you have an excellent record at PharmTech, which makes your recent sales figures all the more striking. If you don't mind, I'd like to review all of this month's contacts case by case and see if we can't figure out what's really going wrong in each particular instance."

c. "Bob, you have an excellent record at PharmTech, which makes your recent sales figures all the more striking. And, because of your history of great performance, I need to be very honest with you. I'm concerned when I see someone's performance decline so sharply. Perhaps it's time we think about moving you

to a different job. I want to help you get what's right-
fully yours without damaging the overall performance of the division."

3. You're the owner of a family restaurant and you're looking for a new manager. Your first interviewee has managed different kinds of restaurants for over 20 years.
When you sit down to interview her, the first thing you
say (after she hands you her resume and you engage in
some obligatory small talk) is:

   a. "Why don't you walk me through your resume and
   tell me something about your specific responsibilities and duties at each of your past positions?"

   b. "Why don't we just put your resume aside for a few
   minutes and you can tell me a bit about your first-
   ever work experience."

   c. "Before we walk through your qualifications, do you
   have any questions about the position you're interviewing for?"

4. One of your employees, Bob, comes to you to complain
about a co-worker, Sally. After he finishes his complaint,
however, he asks you not to mention it or do anything
about it. You respond:

   a. "Bob, if you have a problem with Sally that could possibly affect service to the customer, then you've put
   me in an awkward spot by asking me to not do anything. I'm sorry, but I will have to look into this situation with each of you individually."

   b. "Bob, if that's how you want it, fine. I won't do anything, but neither will I hold this against Sally. I'm
   not going to tarnish her reputation based on
   hearsay."

   c. "Well Bob, if you have this problem with Sally, I'm
   afraid I'm going to bring you both together to
   discuss it. I can't have two of my employees running
   away from each other. We've got to sit down like
   adults and straighten this thing out."

Use the Following Scenario for Questions 5 to 8

You've just been appointed head of a new five-person reengineering project team for the manufacturing division of a
large furniture company, and you have six months to accomplish specific results. The job is not impossible, but it will
require quick and decisive action. Four people have been
assigned to your team, and their attitudes range from enthusiasm to hostility. Your first job as project leader is to talk
with and motivate each person to achieve the team's goals,
although your supervisor has told you that you can, if necessary, remove people from the team.

5. Ann, the first person you talk to, is very excited about
   the project and looking forward to starting. She is moving up quickly within the company and views this project as a way to further prove her mettle. When you ask
   her how she feels about your tight deadline, she says: "I
   think we can make it, but we've all got to get on board. I
   know that I'm ready to go and I'm really looking forward to the opportunity to make some good contributions." In response to this you say:
   a. "Thanks for the input. It's always good to have such
      wonderful enthusiasm involved in a project. But,
      remember that we will all have to work together as a
      team on this. We've just got to be mindful of the
      temptation to go for the individual glory."
   b. "Thanks for the input. I'll be letting you know what
      role you'll be playing sometime this week."
   c. "Thanks for the input. It's always good to have such
      enthusiasm involved with a project like this. I'm
      looking forward to your playing an important role as
      we go forward."

6. The second person you meet with is Bob. He is moder-
   ately enthusiastic about the project but seems to have
   some concerns about the deadline. He's always been a
   very dependable person, but he's never been a shining

star or a real risk-taker. When you ask him what his feelings are regarding the tight deadline, he says: "I do like the assignment, but I'm worried that we might not have enough time to do it right. And I'm not sure we have the resources we need. But, you know, Ann seems to really have a handle on things." In response to this you say:

a. "Well, that's an interesting concern, but I really don't think you need to be worried about it. We have everything under control, and I just know the team is going to work out great. I know that Ann feels the way that I do, so why don't you talk to her and get her reactions to things before we have our first group meeting."

b. "I understand your concern, but I'm very glad you like the assignment. I'll bet if you and Ann work together as the core of the team we can make it."

c. "Thanks for the analysis and the input. Unfortunately, we're all stuck with the deadline and the resources. I wish there was something I could do about it, but you know the guys upstairs only give us what they *think* is necessary, not what really *might* be necessary."

7. The third person you meet with is Ralph, who lives by the code of the *shrug:* who knows, who cares. He's really indifferent to the project as a whole and doesn't seem to want to exert any energy to help it along. When you ask him what his feelings are on the tight deadline you all face, he says: "Well, I don't know . . . I'm just not sure. It's not the project so much as I just don't see how it's possible to pull it off in such a short time." In response to this you say:

a. "I can understand your concern. You've worked with Ann and Bob, right? They're both pretty optimistic and I think we should get together with them to identify our concerns and prepare an action plan. We'll need to work together pretty closely to take advantage of our team potential to reach this goal. It's certainly important to all of us here."

b. "I can understand your concern. Why don't you just go see Ann and Bob and let them explain things to you. Tell them all of your concerns and let them react. They're really ready to take action and can steer you in the right direction."

c. "I'm interested to learn more about your reservations. Why don't you walk me through your specific issues one by one and we'll see which ones we should address."

8. The last person you talk with is Carly. She is downright hostile to being part of this team. When you ask her what her feelings are regarding the tight deadline you are all faced with, she says: "Honestly, I think it's impossible. We're being set up to fail. I don't feel good about working on this project. And I can't see how we can possibly pull this thing off." In response to this you say:

a. "Well, it's certainly your right to feel that way. I think we can succeed wonderfully, but if you don't want to be a part of this, you can leave. I'm authorized to let people go and I think that in your case, this is probably the best thing for everyone."

b. "Well, I appreciate your candor. You know I value your opinion and we both know it's vitally important to build a cohesive team. Would you think about what potential obstacles we ought to watch out for, and prepare a list for discussion? I think we need to be very concrete about what we say and do. The stakes are pretty high."

c. "Well, if you were in my position, what would you do? It's all well and good for you to just sit there and be a negative influence, but I don't have that luxury. So, if you were me, what would you do? We're all stuck in this so we might as well accept reality."

9. You're the manager of a clothing store in a local mall. One day, when you are working with only one other person, you notice that the store is filled with customers and that your one employee is in the back assembling a display. To correct this, you go say to your employee:

   a. "Why are you hanging out back here while we have a store full of customers? We are here to serve, not to assemble displays. From now on, if anything gets in the way of your serving customers, let me know immediately."

   b. "Who told you to come back here to assemble displays? Was it those vendors? Let me know the next time they come in because there is no way I'm letting those people dictate how to run things around here. If they want the displays up, let them put them up."

   c. "Can you take care of that display later? We've got a store full of customers right now. Ask me about this display after this rush dies down a little."

10. If you bring two or more employees together to discuss a conflict and you are unable to help them reach a consensus initially, the best course of action would be to:

    a. Adjourn the meeting for a day or so.

    b. Keep the meeting in session until a consensus is reached.

    c. Adjourn the meeting and decide on a course of action yourself.

11. You have to conduct an evaluation interview for one of your employees, Tony. The most effective way to ensure that any improvements you suggest to him are taken seriously and actually receive his full attention would be to:

    a. Have you and Tony fill out an evaluation form rating his performance.

    b. Have you alone fill out an evaluation form rating Tony's performance.

    c. Have Tony alone fill out an evaluation form rating his performance.

12. When conducting an initial hiring interview, it's best to organize the seating arrangements for the interviewer and the interviewee as follows:

    a. In an office or conference room and face to face (across a desk or table) for a formal, businesslike feel.

    b. In an office or conference room with the chairs arranged side by side or face to face (not separated by a desk or table) in a relaxed, informal fashion.

    c. Out to lunch or dinner in a friendly, casual setting.

13. When undertaking large-scale organizational change, the best course of action is to:

    a. Take action as soon as a general direction is established and fine-tune as you go.

    b. Do a thorough assessment of your current position, then mobilize for action.

    c. Do a complete assessment of your current position, then don't take any action until you have support from everyone in the organization.

14. When you bring two or more employees together to discuss a conflict, it's most effective for you to function in the following role:

    a. Control the discussion and draw very specific bits of information from each participant.

    b. Remain hands off—just make sure that the meeting doesn't get too far out of hand.

    c. Ask questions and draw information from each participant, but let them have some free-flowing discussion between themselves.

15. When conducting hiring interviews, the most useful format for gathering information about a number of different candidates is to:
    a. Use a very structured format, with a list of core questions to be asked of each applicant.
    b. Use a format that traces each individual applicant's history as guided by questions from the interviewer.
    c. Use a very loose format, allowing each individual applicant to highlight his or her most important achievements.

16. When discussing signs of negative changes in a subordinate's performance (such as poor concentration, pessimism, lethargy, indecisiveness, finger-pointing, fatigue, and so on) it's best to:
    a. Discuss these signs only as they relate to work performance.
    b. Discuss these signs and how they might impact home life, work life, and any other areas.
    c. Steer clear of any part of the problems' causes; discuss only how to make positive changes to specific behaviors.

17. A co-worker or subordinate, who you've heard through the grapevine has had some very significant personal problems at home for about a month, approaches you for advice. Your best response is to:
    a. Listen to his or her problems and then offer counsel and guidance based upon your knowledge and experience.
    b. Listen to his or her problems and then offer some possible avenues for seeking counsel and guidance from a professional.
    c. Tell him or her you're probably not the best person to talk to and that he or she should go right to a professional for help.

18. When conducting an initial hiring interview, it's best to spend the following amount of time listening versus talking:

   a. More time talking than listening.

   b. More time listening than talking.

   c. The same amount of time listening and talking.

Use the Following Scenario for Questions 19 to 22

You're a lab manager at a genetics testing company, and it's time for you to conduct some annual performance appraisals. The first person you speak with is Frank. Frank has been a relatively steady and good employee, but he does occasionally communicate a sarcastic attitude and has been known to make snide remarks in staff meetings.

19. Your best approach in setting up Frank's performance appraisal is to:

   a. Arrange one meeting with Frank: Explain the review process and perform his evaluation at this meeting.

   b. Arrange two meetings with Frank: one to explain the review process, and a second to perform the evaluation.

   c. Meet with Frank and involve him in arranging the evaluation process according to his schedule.

20. You explain to Frank, "We're going to evaluate service and the specific behavior it takes to deliver it. In consultation with customers, employees, and the board, the company has committed itself to examining distinct categories of performance. These are: first, individual service to customers; second, service to team members; third, stewardship, including attendance and efficient use of staff and resources; and, last, technical competency in specific work roles." To this, Frank replies sarcastically, "Well, doesn't evaluation really just come down to whether you know how to play the game?" You reply:

a. "Not at all. In fact I'm a bit surprised that you asked me that. We've committed ourselves to a pretty honorable path of commitment to the customer and, in fact, any political game playing of the sort that you're talking about won't be tolerated. You need to think of yourself as being in the front lines of service just like a doctor in a hospital. Your service to our customers is as important as the doctor's treatment of a patient."

b. "I don't really think so. Does it seem that way? Because I've always felt that we're like doctors in a hospital. We're responsible for treating our patients with the best care possible and giving all of our energy to the patient."

c. "Good question. You tell me, Frank. Let's consider a different setting than our own, say a hospital. Would you want to be in the hands of a brilliant doctor who doesn't show up? Or a nurse who tells you to bite the bullet when you ask for pain medication? Or a lab tech who forgets to share information with your physician regarding blood tests?"

21. In response to what you've just told him, Frank continues his sarcastic and snide remarks: "I can see what you mean about a hospital, but I'm not likely to kill anyone from my chair in this lab." You say:

a. "I see your point, but you may be underestimating your importance to the team and our customers. Could the results of your tests reveal a health problem for the public? If you didn't accurately perform the tests, could our clients sue the company for failure to fulfill our responsibilities? If the results were wrong or late, would our co-workers be put in a huge jam when preparing reports? What would be your answers to these questions, Frank?"

   b. "Listen, Frank, we're rapidly reaching the point where your attitude is inappropriate and, frankly, insubordinate. I would suggest to you that before going any further, you pause and rethink your attitude. I'm going to take a few minutes myself before I let this incident unnecessarily color my evaluation of you."

   c. "Frank, I'm sorry you feel this way. Don't you see how important you are to the team? Without every one of us giving 110 percent we're just not going to make it. What can I say to convince you that your role is just as important as that doctor's role?"

22. The most defensible evaluation form is:

   a. A very general form with lots of specific notes from the evaluator.

   b. A very specific form with few written notes from the evaluator.

   c. No form at all, with extensive written notes from the evaluator.

23. When your employees are faced with significant personal problems, the best way for you to maintain their performance on the job is to:

   a. Give them a few days off to sort out whatever they need to, but don't let them forget that one of the purposes of taking a brief hiatus is to improve their on-the-job performance.

   b. Let them sort out whatever they have to on their own time; help them maintain a sense of discipline and structure while they're at work.

   c. Give them as much time off as they need to achieve real, long-term closure for whatever the issue is.

24. When addressing productivity problems, the starting point for discussion with associates should be the question:

   a. How do you feel?

    b. What are you doing?

    c. Where's the problem?

25. If, when undertaking large-scale change, you have a contingent of people who are unwilling to participate, your best course of action is to:

    a. Strive to get them all on board; they could derail your process later.

    b. Isolate them from the people spearheading the change process; make an effort to remove them from the organization now.

    c. Offer them the opportunity to participate, but do not take any significant effort to bring them along; focus on the people with positive energy.

26. The central issue leaders need to address to ensure high levels of teamwork and productivity is:

    a. The way work is organized.

    b. Performance incentives (financial or otherwise).

    c. Team and interpersonal skills training for employees.

27. One of your employees, Tom, comes to you and says, "Jon is really screwing up on the job. He's messed up three orders in the past two days. If something isn't done about him soon, we could start losing contracts." You respond by saying, "I hear you," to which Tom angrily replies, "I've heard that before. Are you going to do something or not?" You say:

    a. "I understand that you're angry at Jon. Your job is to handle the orders and tell me about any problems you may have. You did that. Now it's my problem. Let me handle my job and you do yours, okay?"

    b. "I understand that you're angry at Jon. I will speak with him and take care of the problem you've just told me about as soon as we're done here."

    c. "Listen, Tom, this is my problem and I will handle it as I see fit. I will not do this on your schedule or anyone else's. I will do what I think is appropriate when I think it's appropriate. And, frankly, if that means I don't take action on your allegations, then so be it."

28. As a leader, when you make a mistake it's best to:

a. Admit your mistake before addressing a solution; it's important to show your employees that you're human without unnecessarily weakening your leadership position.

b. Move on quickly without admitting your mistake; once you allow yourself to be treated like your employees, you will no longer be regarded as a strong leader.

c. Admit your mistake and address a solution immediately; it's important that your employees see that not only does everyone make mistakes, but that everyone is held accountable to the same principles.

Use the Following Scenario for Questions 29 to 32

You're a real estate agent and you believe that you have found a perfect match between a family looking to buy and a house for sale in an attractive suburban neighborhood.

29. Your first order of business is to discuss the selling price with Niles, the present owner of the house. You initiate this discussion by saying, "Niles, I need to be sure I really understand your needs and requirements regarding price. May I ask, what's your bottom line? What must you get?" To this, Niles says, "As much as we can." Your response is:

a. "Well, we did a market analysis of the area, so we have a starting price. But we may be able to sell it for more to a couple I've got lined up. Let's highlight the repairs and improvements you've made here and see if they go for that."

    b. "Well, let me give you a market analysis we completed which includes the sale of a home just up the street. We believe that yours should sell for about $10,000 more because of size and condition."

    c. "Well, believe me, Niles, you and I share the same concern. We did a market analysis of the area and some of the recent sales on the street, but we shouldn't limit ourselves to that just yet. Why don't I see where I can get with this prospect and we'll see where that takes us."

30. Next, you have a meeting with the interested couple, Mark and Jean. They have two children, ages 13 and 16, and as you think about what kinds of requirements they might have, you note that the number of bathrooms might be an issue. You also know that both parents work full-time and their kids will most likely have to spend some time alone at home, so they're probably concerned about the safety of the neighborhood. Niles's house fits the bill in these areas quite nicely and you'd like to have Mark and Jean see the house. You get together with them for lunch, and after some small talk you say:

    a. "I've thought about your situation and it seems that you're really going to need some basic things addressed. First, because of your two kids, you'll probably need a place with good bathroom space. And second, because you both work, you'll probably want some assurances that this place is pretty safe. Right?"

    b. "I need to have an understanding of your day-to-day needs to identify houses for you to look at. What are your most important considerations?"

    c. "I've thought about what you might need in a house and I think I've found just the place. It has everything I think you need, and I think it's going to be a great fit."

31. After discussing some specifics with Jean and Mark, you get the sense that Jean has some concerns other than the physical layout of the house. Although she hasn't said so, you sense that she's even more concerned about long-term issues like the house's resale value. You address this by saying:

a. "I'm getting the sense that you have some concerns about the house as a financial investment. You don't need to be worried about that because this area is just fantastic. We've had great resale values for years and our current market analyses don't show any sign of dropping off."

b. "What is it that you ultimately want to get out of this home? What are your real hopes and expectations?"

c. "I know that you probably have some other areas of concern you'd like to address, but can I suggest that we put those on hold until we actually see some homes? I think we want to keep a clear mind about how the house will actually work for your living requirements before we address some of the larger issues."

32. Finally, after you address all of these issues, your conversation starts to wind down. Before you formally end your meeting, however, you remember that the local school system might be an issue to them. You say:

a. "Just one more point before we go. The schools around here are really quite good and I'm sure your children will fit in just fine. I haven't seen any kids yet that haven't."

b. "Over the next few days, why don't you drive around the area and take a look at the schools. You'll have a nice time and you can just fit that in at your own pace."

c. "Are there any special needs that you want me to consider in looking at houses, such as schools?"

33. When an organization is about to undertake any kind of significant change (from layoffs to restructuring to mergers), the best course of action for senior leadership is to:

a. Decide on the best course of action for the organization, and when implementation is under way, involve the front lines bit by bit as needed.

    b. Inform the front lines as soon as the need for significant change is discovered. Involve the front lines early and often throughout the change process, while keeping firm control of the basic direction in which you want the organization to head.

    c. Inform the front lines as soon as the need for significant change is discovered. Let the front lines determine the direction the organization should head and allow them to share authority in the ultimate decision-making process.

34. You're the management head of a contract negotiating unit for your local hospital and you've been charged with resolving some outstanding issues with Linda, the head of the local nurses union. You begin the meeting by saying, "Linda, thank you for the opportunity to meet to address our remaining challenges. What's your analysis of our current standing and today's objectives?" Her response is, "Well, frankly, my challenge is explaining to my people why they should agree to anything when they don't know what management's plans are for the future. If we sign the three-year agreement and you merge with the hospital system down the street, then where are we?" You reply:

    a. "I understand. You're saying that your people don't know why they should agree to a plan for their future when they don't know a major piece of the plan— namely, the future for the hospital as a whole. Is that right?"

    b. "Well frankly, Linda, I'm not sure you're really getting the big picture. Your people don't have much of an option in this case. The executive team is going to do whatever they're going to do, regardless of what your constituents think. However, if you want the agreement for as long as it's good, we'd love to have you along."

    c. "Listen, if you need some other kinds of assurances, I'll try to get those assurances. We will do whatever we need to do to make the union feel more comfortable with the agreement."

35. You are approached by one of your employees who is having a serious problem with another of your employees. The first thing you should do is:

    a. Bring them together to discuss their conflict.

    b. Talk with each person individually to do your own assessment of the conflict.

    c. Stay out of it and let them resolve the issue themselves.

36. When one of your subordinates starts evidencing negative changes in performance (such as poor concentration, pessimism, lethargy, indecisiveness, blaming others, fatigue, and so on) it's best to:

    a. Discuss the situation with that person as soon as you see a slight change (before a specific incident occurs).

    b. Discuss the situation as soon as possible after a specific incident occurs.

    c. Wait until you have more than one specific incident or confirmation from other co-workers to back up your assertions before you discuss this with your subordinate.

■ ANSWER KEY

➤ Directions

Using the following key, compare your answers to the ones listed. For every correct answer, give yourself 1 point in the Points column. For all wrong answers, give yourself 0 points in the Points column. Once you're finished scoring, total your points in the space marked Total.

Question number and answer	Your answer	Points
1. A		
2. A		
3. B		
4. A		
5. C		
6. B		
7. A		
8. B		
9. C		
10. A		
11. A		
12. B		
13. B		
14. C		
15. B		
16. A		
17. B		
18. B		
19. B		
20. C		
21. A		
22. B		
23. A		
24. B		
25. C		
26. A		
27. A		
28. C		
29. B		
30. B		
31. B		
32. C		
33. B		
34. A		
35. B		
36. B		

Total: _____

■ INTERPRETING YOUR LIQ SELF-ASSESSMENT RESULTS

➤ Directions

Using your Total score from the Answer Key, find your scoring range to determine your overall Leadership IQ.

For a more complete assessment, and an in-depth, role-by-role scoring analysis, please call E. C. Murphy, Ltd., at 1-800-922-5005.

Score	Leadership IQ
33–36	**High superior:** You demonstrate extensive knowledge and practical understanding of the course of action chosen by exceptional leaders.
27–32	**Superior:** You demonstrate significant knowledge and practical understanding of the course of action chosen by exceptional leaders.
20–26	**High average:** You demonstrate basic knowledge and practical understanding of the course of action chosen by exceptional leaders.
9–19	**Average:** You demonstrate partial knowledge and practical understanding of the course of action chosen by exceptional leaders.
0–8	**Low average:** You demonstrate cursory and intermittent knowledge and practical understanding of the course of action chosen by exceptional leaders.

■ THE LEADERSHIP IQ DEVELOPMENT GUIDE

➤ Directions

Once you have obtained your overall LIQ score, you're ready to target specific areas for improvement.

If your answer for a question was wrong, or if it was right but you're not sure why, reference the specific chapter and page number listed next to the question number. This will serve as your index to successful workleaders' rationale in choosing a particular course of action.

Once you've targeted and researched specific areas for improvement using this guide, we recommend that you read the entire book in sequence to get a full sense of the synergies high LIQ leaders achieve as they approach excellence in their work roles.

28.   *See Chapter 7: The Healer, page 187.*
29.   *See Chapter 6: The Negotiator, page 147.*
30.   *See Chapter 6: The Negotiator, page 148.*
31.   *See Chapter 6: The Negotiator, page 150.*
32.   *See Chapter 6: The Negotiator, page 153.*
33.   *See Chapter 9: The Synergizer, page 230.*
34.   *See Chapter 6: The Negotiator, page 156.*
35.   *See Chapter 8: The Protector, page 203.*
36.   *See Chapter 7: The Healer, page 173.*

Bibliography

Connors, Roger, Tom Smith, and Craig Hickman. *The Oz Principle: Getting Results Through Individual and Organizational Accountability*. Englewood Cliffs, N.J.: Prentice-Hall, 1994.

Devansen, Chandran D. S. *The Making of the Mahatma*. Madras: G. M. Salis, 1969.

Friedel, Frank. *Franklin D. Roosevelt: A Rendezvous with Destiny*. New York: Little, Brown and Company, 1990.

Glasser, William. *Reality Therapy: A New Approach to Psychiatry*. New York: Harper & Row, Publishers, 1965.

Hobbs, Joseph Patrick. *Dear General: Eisenhower's Wartime Letters to Marshall*. Baltimore, Md.: The Johns Hopkins Press, 1971.

Jakab, Peter L. *Visions of a Flying Machine*. Washington, D.C.: Smithsonian Institution Press, 1990.

Keller, Helen. *Teacher: Anne Sullivan Macy*. Garden City, N.Y.: Doubleday, 1955.

McClelland, David. *The Achieving Society*. New York: The Free Press, 1967.

Maddi, Salvatore. *Personality Theories: A Comparative Analysis*. Pacific Grove, Calif.: Brooks-Cole Publishing Company, 1989.

Murphy, Emmett C. *Forging the Heroic Organization*. Englewood Cliffs, N.J.: Prentice-Hall, 1994.

———. *The Genius of Sitting Bull: 13 Heroic Strategies for Today's Business Leaders*. Englewood Cliffs, N.J.: Prentice-Hall, 1993.

———. *Leadership IQ: A Technical Report on the Research Methodology and Assessments*. Amherst, N.Y.: E.C. Murphy, Ltd., 1996.

Oates, Stephen B. *With Malice Toward None: A Life of Abraham Lincoln*. New York: Harper and Row Publishers, 1977.

Schein, Edgar H. *Process Consultation*. Reading, Mass.: Addison-Wesley Publishing, 1988.

Seligman, Martin E. P. *Learned Optimism*. New York: Simon & Shuster, 1991.

Silva, Michael. *Overdrive: Managing in Crisis-Filled Times*. New York: John Wiley & Sons, 1995.

Index

To learn more about the ideas and techniques in this book, contact:

E.C. Murphy, Ltd.
4246 Ridge Lea Road, Suite 80
Amherst, NY 14226
1-800-922-5005